THE
TOMMY JOHN
STORY

THE TOMMY JOHN STORY

**Tommy and Sally John
with Joe Musser**

Foreword by Tom Lasorda

Fleming H. Revell Company
Old Tappan, New Jersey

Bible quotations are from the King James Version of the Bible.

Library of Congress Cataloging in Publication Data

John, Tommy.
    The Tommy John story.

    1. John, Tommy.   2.   Baseball players—United
States—Biography.   3.   Religion and sports.
I. John, Sally, joint author.   II.   Musser, Joe,
joint author.   III.   Title.
GV865.J58A37   796.357′092′4   [B]   78-17705
ISBN 0-8007-0923-3

To my Dad
Thomas E. John, Sr.

Contents

Foreword

As manager of the Los Angeles Dodgers, I try to build a team of togetherness. And that's what we built on the 1977 Dodger team. Having a young man like Tommy John pitch for me is every manager's dream. He's a man who gives of himself at all times, an unselfish pitcher who ignores his own individual achievements and is solely concerned with team effort. Tommy John is a tremendous athlete and competitor, but above all he's an outstanding young man.

I was there in Dodger Stadium on that dreadful day Tommy John, pitching against the Montreal Expos, walked off the mound into the clubhouse. The doctor examined him and we all knew Tommy had done something seriously wrong to his arm. Later, he faced a difficult, uncertain, and experimental operation. Everyone, including the doctors, thought Tommy John would never pitch again. But through sheer determination, his complete faith in Christ, and the drive within himself, Tommy John believed he *would* pitch again.

Through agonizing hard work, self-confidence, and a full year of struggle, Tommy was driven by the will to accomplish something impossible.

The following year—1976—Tommy John won 10 ball games for the Los Angeles Dodgers, was voted the Comeback Player of the Year, and received the Fred Hutchinson Award for Courage.

In 1977, Tommy John absolutely amazed baseball fans with something that was simply unbelievable—he won 20 ball games for the National League champions, the Los Angeles Dodgers, and finished second in the balloting for the coveted Cy Young Award. No one knows better than I do what a tremendous accomplishment this was! Truly it's great evidence of what it takes to have confidence, faith in God, and a tremendous amount of desire. Tommy John is already an inspiration to thousands who know of his struggle and comeback.

His story will be an inspiration to countless others who need just such encouragement. When things get tough and you think everything is against you, this little saying will help you—just as Tommy John thought when things looked tough for him:

BECAUSE GOD DELAYS
DOES NOT MEAN THAT GOD DENIES.

Tommy John accomplished something possibly no one else could have done, but even he will tell you that he only accomplished it because of his deep faith in Jesus Christ.

TOM LASORDA

1

From Little League to Class A Ball

Of the 24 million boys who aspired to professional baseball that summer of 1953, perhaps only a handful were as serious and determined as ten-year-old Tommy John, Jr., growing up in Terre Haute, Indiana.

The boy and his dad both loved baseball. Tommy John, Sr., had been a good ballplayer in his youth and active as a young man in semipro baseball. On evenings or weekends, the wives and girl friends of the ballplayers packed picnic lunches and went to a local park or stadium for a game. His dad played shortstop, third base, and pitched a little. He earned the then-handsome sum of twenty-five dollars for each game.

However, Tommy's dad gave up the game when his daughter, Marilyn, was born. With the insecurities and risks of semipro ball, he couldn't jeopardize his family's future with an injury and decided to quit.

His interest was renewed when he saw the love his *son* had for the game, however. With what seemed to be unusual coordination for a youngster, Tommy began to pitch as an eight-year-old in the Spencer Park Recreational League. The times when he wasn't pitching, the boy played first base or in the outfield. Tommy's dad, now his coach, taught him the fundamentals of the game, including how to bunt, field, and throw, as well as pitch.

When Tommy was ten, his dad—a Little League coach—let his son join the team. He was a contrast to many Little League coaches. He believed boys should *enjoy* baseball, that the game should be fun. It never occurred to him to pressure the youngsters—to really get on them about the game. Instead of yelling and screaming and demanding beyond their capabilities, Tommy's dad simply instructed the boys and let them grow according to their individual efforts and abilities.

Tommy's dad was employed by the Public Service Company of Indiana. He and his partner often talked about baseball when driving the company truck.

"Al, I've been thinking," Mr. John said one day. "Why couldn't a fellow develop talent in sports the way a guy might work at music or study piano?"

"Maybe so," his partner answered.

"You know, Al, I think I'll work with my boy. He loves baseball. Maybe he's got only average talent, but if he works hard—like a fellow would study piano and practice—he might make something of it."

"Could be, Tom. Could be."

One day Dad watched out the kitchen window over a cup of coffee, as his son struggled with a wheelbarrow full of dirt, almost spilling the load several times before reaching the backyard.

"What's he doing?" asked Tommy's mom.

"I think he's fixing to build himself a pitcher's mound," replied Dad, who quickly sipped the last of his coffee and hurried outside to help his son.

After a few hours and several more wheelbarrow loads, a pitcher's mound began to take shape. The boy and his dad measured off the correct distance and dug a spot for the home plate. Then they created a narrow strike zone—two parallel vertical poles stuck into the ground with a pair of horizontal string lines—a marking for the knees and shoulders of a batter. Then they connected two vertical strings to the horizontal ones, completing the target. "Son, the main idea for a pitcher is to throw strikes. No matter how hard you throw, if you can't throw strikes you will never be successful. The idea of the string idea is to get you accustomed to throwing strikes."

Now it was time to try it out. Dad took an old bucket of baseballs out of the garage, and Tommy threw them at the target. This routine and practice continued for hours—days—at a time.

The seasons came and went. Tommy and his sister, Marilyn, vacationed with Mom and Dad to other parts of the country, as well as Canada. Between trips, however, young Tommy spent his time perfecting the mechanics of baseball, with a few exceptions.

"But I want to pitch," the boy had argued with his dad. "I want to learn to throw curves."

Mr. John shook his head slowly. "It's too soon, son. Your arm isn't ready. You just keep working on the fundamentals. Don't try to rush things. Let's wait a year or two."

These couple of years seemed to go ever so slowly to Tommy. Yet, he respected his father's advice. He practiced seriously and read all the books he could find about pitching. All through his elementary and junior-high school years his dad would be Tommy's only real coach.

One day, Tommy's dad called him and explained as they got in the car, "I thought we'd go visit Arley Andrews."

Tommy's heart began to pound. Arley Andrews! A Terre Haute resident, Andrews preceded Tommy at Gerstmeyer High School by several years and had played professional baseball in the Philadelphia Phillies organization.

"Arley can teach you the way the Phillies showed him how to throw a curve ball," smiled Dad.

The day was a high point in the young boy's life. *A personal pitching lesson from a real pro!* In his quiet Southern Indiana drawl, Arley explained the mechanics. Then he demonstrated the pitch step-by-step. Then he uncorked the ball toward Dad who was catching for them. *Whap!* There was the distinctive crack of the ball smacking the glove which to the seasoned observer denotes speed, trajectory, and accuracy.

Whap! Again the ball curved to its target.

And again. *Whap!*

"Now you try it, Tommy."

Tommy took the baseball in his hand. In Arley's brawny fingers it looked small. He struggled to wrap his fingers around the ball as Arley had instructed. "Closer—keep your fingers closer together. Like this."

Tommy tried to copy Arley's motion but felt slightly awkward. The big ballplayer had made it look so easy. He uncorked the pitch and it curved—but wildly—in front of his dad who captured it in the dust.

"It's okay. You've got to get more control. Keep trying," encouraged Arley.

His second pitch seemed more reassuring. But the *whump* sound of it hitting the glove made him realize it still wasn't right.

Arley was patient and gave the right advice. It wasn't too long before the small sandlot was echoing with the *whap* of balls striking the glove, as the young boy learned the pitch.

Tommy was taught to pitch curves and fast balls. These two pitches would help his Babe Ruth League team to the state finals and the state championship. In high school and in American Legion ball his pitching earned trophies and honors for this Southern Indiana teenager. Tommy pitched 2 no-hitters during his 2 years in American Legion ball. The first no-hitter was July 2, 1960, against the Marshall, Illinois, American Legion team. His second no-hitter was against the Linton, Indiana, American Legion team on July 22, 1960. During his four years of high-school baseball and American Legion ball, he averaged 16 strikeouts a game in a 21-out game. His strikeout high was 23 out of 27 outs. During this time, including the 2 no-hitters, he had 12 one-hitters and several two-hitters. Needless to say, scouts from all over the country were hearing about Tommy John.

Bill Welch, Tommy's future American Legion baseball coach, recalls an incident which he thought might have ended the young pitcher's career before it started. Tommy's Babe Ruth League team was playing an exhibition game with the Bill Welch-coached Wayne Newton Post #546 Legion team. Playing the older and more experienced Legion players would be good experience for Tommy's Babe Ruth League All-Star team and would help them in the State Final Championships.

The game was in the first inning of play when a freak incident happened. A baseball was hit very hard toward Tommy. He instinctively put his hand up to stop the ball which struck his pitching hand. Welch ran over from his third base coach's box to the young boy and saw the bone jutting through the skin of his thumb, and the thumb was dangling backwards, held only by skin and tendon. A compound dislocation and fracture prevented Tommy from pitching in the regional and state finals and going on to the national series, but the finger healed by the next season.

During the wintertime, Tommy played basketball. In fact, basketball is *the* Hoosier sport—the one its natives take most seriously. Varsity basketball coach Howard Sharpe was glad that Tommy excelled at this sport also. (Sharpe was also the varsity baseball coach.) In fact, by the time he would graduate from Gerstmeyer, he'd receive some thirty-five athletic scholarship offers to colleges who wanted him to play—*basketball!* His record of 47 points in a single game—one more than the former record holder, Arley Andrews—has never been broken at Gerstmeyer. Yet baseball was Tommy's real love, so basketball was always kept in balance. Baseball was kept in its proper perspective as far as Tommy's schoolwork was concerned. His grades didn't suffer—he was valedictorian in his graduating class of 225.

Tommy took sports, his studies, everything—seriously. He succeeded at everything he tried. He started a doughnut route one summer, taking orders for and delivering fresh hot bakery doughnuts to customers twice a week, earning the then-handsome sum of thirty dollars weekly. He was always the high salesperson in the Gerstmeyer magazine drives and in his senior year he was the high salesperson for the school, which has over a thousand students.

Tommy's parents had given him the things they felt were important, including an early desire to attend church and Sunday school. These values and a personal Christian faith were part of his character from these earliest school days, and would guide his growing-up decisions later on. His parents were equally proud of Tommy's sister, Marilyn, named "Singer of the Year" in national competition in Minneapolis, and earning her an audition with the Metropolitan Opera.

Tommy's high-school baseball record was 28 wins, 2 losses. He lost both games to their archrival across the state line, Danville, Illinois. He averaged, for four years of high school baseball, 3.8 hits per game—quite an impressive average.

The first loss was a disappointing shutout. The opposing pitcher was Steve Kelly, who later signed as a professional in the Kansas City organization. Gerstmeyer coach Howard Sharpe had told him before the game, "Now remember, Tommy—there will be a lot of baseball scouts here today. Even though you're only fifteen years old, they'll make notes on any promising boy so they can keep track of his progress until he graduates."

"Well, Son, you did your best and that's all that counts." Dad was always one of the first to come to him after a game. Win or lose, his attitude was the same.

"Yeah, but, you know, Dad," declared Tommy, "I really wanted to win this one."

"It doesn't matter," explained Dad. You see that man in the blue jacket over there?"

"Yeah . . . ."

"Well, he's a scout for Cleveland," smiled Dad, "and he came over and told me he wants to keep an eye on you. He asked me all about your grades, sports, school, and all . . . ."

"Really?"

Dad nodded proudly. "Yessir . . . says they're going to keep an eye on Tommy John. There are scouts interested in him here from Pittsburgh, Philadelphia, Saint Louis, Chicago, Kansas City, Chicago, Milwaukee, San Francisco—and the California Angels."

Two years later, tall and muscular seventeen-year-old Tommy John lost his second game to Danville, 2–1. Once more, scouts were in the stands. Again he was disappointed.

"No reason to be too upset," said Cleveland scout John Schulte, who introduced himself to Tommy's parents after the game. "A 28–2 high-school record is one to be very proud of. Besides, it's the 'win' side of the column that convinced us to offer Tommy a major league baseball contract—not the two losses."

Tommy's father could hardly speak. "Wh-What? a contract?"

"Our offer probably will be just one of many, Mr. John."

Schulte's conversation proved to be prophetic. Many ball clubs approached the Johns with fantastic offers. Bonus money in amounts almost unheard of to the modest Midwest family were being discussed.

Out of all the teams scouting him, Cleveland offered the highest. "Cleveland offered thirty-five thousand dollars just to sign," Tommy excitedly told his mother later.

"Imagine that, Honey!" Tommy's dad said to his wife. "Why that's over twice what I make in a year!"

"I can't believe it," she bubbled.

Arley Andrews was pleased when he heard the news, and offered some advice from his own experience. "Don't let them have you go all over the country for tryouts. It's better if you make them go on your record and the scouting reports. Let them get into a bidding contest; *then* you sign with the one you believe in most."

Bruce Connatser, a Philadelphia scout and family friend, had followed Tommy's career since he was a fourteen-year-old in Babe Ruth League ball. Mr. and Mrs. John had promised Bruce a final option to bid on a major league contract for Tommy.

Since Cleveland had offered Tommy thirty-five thousand dollars to sign, they told Bruce that Tommy would sign for forty thousand dollars. Bruce checked with Philadelphia and told Mr. John the price was too steep, so Tommy went back to counter Cleveland's offer and signed with the Indians for a forty thousand-dollar bonus and seven hundred dollars-a-month contract.

It was 1961 and upon graduation the tall boy from Terre Haute flew to Dubuque, Iowa, to join Cleveland's farm team. The Dubuque Packers (so named for the city's leading industry, Dubuque Meat Packing Company) were in the Class D Midwest* League.

Cleveland's management planned to start Tommy there and let him get his feet wet in professional baseball in 1961. After a season of Class D ball, in 1962 the plan was to move him up to Class B competition. In 1963, they reasoned, he'd be ready for Class A baseball, followed by the more competitive Triple-A ball in 1964. If all went well, by 1965—in four years—Tommy John would be a major league baseball player.

* Today Class D is comparable to the Class A League. In 1963, Classes B, C, and D were combined into the present Class A organization.

In one of his first workouts with the Cleveland Indians (prior to his signing), the team's pitching coach, Mel Harder, watched Tommy closely. The young pitcher sat down on the bench and mopped perspiration from his head with a thick towel.

"Your pitching mechanics are good—real good," Mel began. "You've had some good training."

"The best," Tommy said. "My dad was my coach."

"Well, every coach has his own approach, but the end result is *does it work?* I want you to pitch the way you always have and we'll see the results, then decide whether we want you to change."

Tommy nodded.

During the '61 season, Tommy was allowed to pitch two exhibition games for the Cleveland Indians. The first was a game against the International League All Stars. Tommy gave up just 1 unearned run in 3 innings of work. In August, he pitched a solid 5 innings against the Cincinnati Reds, the National League champs for 1961. His record was 3–3 at the time. After the game, Frank Funk, an Indian pitcher, congratulated Tommy.

"Your pitching is superb!" he exclaimed. "I can't believe you are just 3–3. If you can pitch well against a great club like the Reds, then you should really tear up a Class D league."

"Gee, thanks, Frank," responded Tommy. "I appreciate your encouragement."

Tommy went back to Dubuque to win 7 and lose 1 after that.

He went 10–4 for the 1961 season. His pitching impressed the club and they moved him up a full year in the schedule. "You're going to skip Class B ball and go right into Class A next season. We're expecting great things from Tommy John!" said his manager.

2

A Dream Comes True

After he established himself as a pitcher in Dubuque, the Cleveland organization sent Tommy to Charleston, West Virginia, in the Eastern League. As a promising prospect in the Cleveland organization, Tommy was promoted to the forty-man spring-training roster, working out with "the big club."

During spring-training workouts in Tucson, Arizona, Tommy had no idea what was expected of him, and felt awkward reporting to the club. Last year he was a high-school boy—now he was working out with the major league greats: Jim "Mudcat" Grant, Joe Adcock, All-Star pitcher Dick Donovan, and his roommate, Jerry Kendall, now the University of Arizona baseball coach. Manager Mel McGaha gave out assignments but more or less assumed everyone knew what to do. Rather than appear slow by asking what he was *supposed* to do, Tommy just copied the other pitchers. When they did calisthenics, so did he; when they jogged, so did he. When another pitcher went for a Coke, Tommy needed a bottle, too.

Steve Jankowski, about nine years older than Tommy, was already a veteran in the game. He'd been injured playing Triple A baseball and his dream of playing in the major leagues was over. Steve stayed on as one of the team's organization men. There are no coaches in the minor leagues, as such, yet, Jankowski seemed to function as one. Tommy had the good fortune of rooming with the older ballplayer who took the young pitcher under his wing.

"Is it true what they say about the Eastern League?" Tommy asked Steve one day.

"What do they say?"

"That most ballplayers from the Eastern League go into the big leagues—more than any other league in baseball."

Steve nodded. "I guess that's true. But a lot of guys get hit hard here and don't make it."

"What about me. Have I got a chance?"

Steve frowned, then nodded. "It's coming . . . but . . . ."

"But, what . . . ?"

"Well, you got great stuff, Tommy," the older ballplayer continued. "Trouble is, you walk too many batters. You don't have to take on the team singlehandedly, you know. Give your fielders a chance to catch the ball. Just go out there and see how many times you can get those guys to hit the ball. Don't be afraid of giving them good pitches. Go up there and say, 'Here's the ball, now hit it!' "

Tommy tried out Steve's suggestion in a game against York, Pennsylvania. Instead of trying to be a strikeout king, Tommy relaxed and just tried to put the ball over the plate. He shut out York 3–0 in 9 innings of superb pitching, striking out 12, without walking a batter. Steve's advice also proved itself over the season.

There was little glamour in this side of baseball. The hopeful young ballplayers worked out strenuously each day. A hectic playing schedule left little time for social activities.

Travel was not the most luxurious, either. The shortest trip between Charleston and the nearest club in the Eastern League was ten hours—by *bus*. The longest trip between cities for games was twenty-four hours.

The long bus trips were eased by occasional stops at the Howard Johnson oases on the Pennsylvania Turnpike. The team left Charleston at midnight, drove all night, then stopped for breakfast about six in the morning.

The bus would pull in to the town about 4:30 in the afternoon and head directly to the motel. There the players would quickly check in, eat, dress, and go straight to the playing field. Often they'd arrive just at game time, with no time for warm-ups or batting practice.

The next morning the players would rise early enough to shower, shave, and be downstairs by 7:00 A.M. This was the time the motel served its continental breakfast (included in the price of the room). To save on the $3.50 daily meal money allowance, Tommy and the others would have coffee and six or seven sweet rolls—enough to tide them over until the bus stopped around noon at a White Castle or McDonald's for the guys to grab a quick burger on their way to the game.

Tommy's competition was tough in the Eastern League, and he faced such stalwarts as Ken Harrelson, Dick Allen, Dave McNally, Luis Tiant, Jim Ray Hart, and Davey Johnson, who were in the league at the same time.

Jankowski's pitching counsel proved to be just what the young hurler needed. Tommy (now sporting the nickname "T.J.") was pitching and winning sensational games.

By July, the Cleveland club's Triple A team in Jacksonville, Florida, was leading the league, but running out of pitchers. Cleveland had called a few pitchers up to their major league club and the vacancies were felt all down the line.

The Jacksonville player-coach, Al Jones, was a catcher who remembered Tommy when he tried out for the Cleveland organization the year before. Jones said to the team's manager, Ben Geraghty, "There's this southpaw kid from Indiana I caught last year in Cleveland. He's with Charleston. He's young, but he can really throw the ball."

"Let's get him down here," Geraghty replied. "We need somebody who can pitch every fifth game."

Tommy had not yet completed his first full year in professional baseball before joining the Jacksonville team. In a sense, he knew he was in over his head, but he enjoyed it and did the job the team management expected.

His first game was in the International League against the Syracuse Chiefs, a Detroit farm club. Tommy was visibly nervous and committed the "deadly sin" of walking hitters. However, he was backed by the good defensive play of his Jacksonville teammates, who helped him recover and win the game. In his next start, against the Rochester Red Wings, Tommy pitched 7 strong innings, leaving the game winning, 3–2. Next, he pitched a 3-hit shutout against the

Columbus Jets. He compiled a 2–2 record with 2 wins in the play-offs.

He did make mistakes, but the team won the league pennant by the end of the season, coinciding with Tommy's improvement and experience. Playing against such greats as Sparky Anderson, Luke Easter, Joe Lonnett, Mickey Lolich, Al Downing, Mel Stottlemyre, Tim McCarver, Willie Stargell, and Bob Bailey helped give him confidence.

That winter, Tommy went home exhilarated and perhaps even a little cocky. He had pitched Triple A baseball—where "Everyone is either a major league prospect or suspect," as the old dugout cliché went. The player was either a bright new star on his way up, or an injured, spent athlete fighting for his baseball career. Both had everything to prove, everything to lose. Competition was intense—but Tommy loved it. The club had projected his reaching Triple A baseball in 1964. It was now 1962, and Tommy was already on a Triple A championship team.

During the off-season Tommy went to Indiana State University, majoring in mathematics, and during the winter he worked out regularly to keep in shape. An old baseball pro told Tommy he could stay years longer in baseball by remaining active year round. Tommy worked out, played basketball and badminton, and ran several miles daily. He felt, too, he was getting good practice for performing under pressure by refereeing volatile Indiana high-school basketball games. He also was a TV color man for Indiana basketball games. He was optimistic by spring-training time—feeling if he had a chance to make the Jacksonville team, maybe he could get the chance he was hoping for—a call to the majors.

Ben Geraghty had other plans, however. He seemed harder on younger players because of his preference for older players. It seemed to Tommy in 1963 that Jacksonville didn't know he even existed. During a six-week period early in the season, Tommy was called upon to pitch just twice, compiling a 1–0 record and hitting a home run.

But Geraghty's apparent indifference and neglect took its toll. A disappointed and angry young pitcher was almost ready to call the

Cleveland management and ask to be sent back to Charleston.

"At least in Charleston I had a chance to pitch. Here I'm wasting away. I've got to pitch," he complained one night during a phone call home to his folks. "That's the only way I can get experience."

Almost as if reading his mind, Tommy heard from Cleveland.

"We want you to report back to Charleston. We need you pitching for us every fourth day, not wasting away on the bench."

Almost immediately, Tommy was back into the routine of long bus rides and Eastern League baseball. The swing from Charleston included cities such as Elmira and Binghamton, New York; York and Reading, Pennsylvania; and as far north as Springfield, Massachusetts. The interminable bus rides around the League were much more bearable in 1963. As a "veteran" of one year, Tommy had friends on the team from the 1962 season. Pete Olsen and Don Schaeffer were two players who were especially close. To make the long, boring trips more tolerable, they played bridge nonstop from the breakfast stop to their arrival in the city where they were to play. The three of them also sneaked their golf clubs along for a clandestine round or two of golf whenever time permitted. Once the trio even rented a car and drove a couple hundred miles to watch the '63 U.S. Open in Brookline, Massachusetts. After walking the course all day, and a brief "meal" of hot dogs, Tommy hurried to the ball park in Springfield and prepared to pitch that night! The escapade did not seem to slow him at all. He pitched a 5–0 shutout.

For nearly three months Tommy pitched for Charleston. He had 11 starts and finished 9–2, pitching 96 innings and giving up only 12 walks—one man on base every 8 innings. Tommy's record and amazingly low earned-run-average of 1.61 once again captured the attention of Cleveland's front office.

"Tommy, Ben Geraghty died—and we've had a shake-up on the Jacksonville team. We've got a new manager and he'll let you pitch. We need you in Florida. Better get your gear ready. You leave right away."

The shake-up was true. A complete transition took place in Jacksonville, as the "young guys" moved in: Mike Cuellar, Duke Sims, Luis Tiant, Sam McDowell and Tommy John were some of those who were to later be big league stars. Finally given their chance, the young ballplayers proved themselves.

"Birdie" Tebbetts was manager of the Cleveland Indians in 1963. Before the season ended that fall, he called Tommy at Jacksonville.

"We like what we see in you, T.J. You've got promise, and you throw pretty well." Then, almost as an afterthought, he added, "We're calling you up to the major leagues. You'll be pitching for the Indians."

"Boy . . . thanks. When do you want me, Skipper?" Tommy stammered. "I'll do my best."

Cleveland finished the season using the young pitcher in the bull pen. His first chance to pitch a major league game came in the Washington, D.C., stadium. Cleveland was losing and Birdie Tebbetts called the bull pen and bellowed, "Send in Tommy John!"

Tommy's stomach knotted. Excitement, fear, exhilaration—and the realization of a lifelong dream was happening at this moment. Tommy John was about to pitch . . . his first major league game!

He strode nervously but quickly to the bull-pen gate to the field. For what seemed to be an eternity, Tommy stood there.

Again the booming command on the bull-pen phone, "Didn't you guys hear me? I said, 'Send in T.J.' "

"We did, Skipper. I don't know what's wrong."

Panic was etched in the face of the young pitcher. Not butterflies for his first game, but the fact that no one had told Tommy how to open the gate onto the field!

Surely I won't have to climb over this ten-foot fence, Tommy said to himself. He reached out and shook the gate and the latch separated and the door opened. Tommy sighed and ran to the mound. The actual pitching would be easy after this! He did superbly, giving up only 1 unearned run in 2 innings.

Tommy pitched 2 more times in relief that year, both times against the Minnesota Twins, without allowing a run. Then he was given an opportunity to start against the California Angels and the ace pitcher, Dean Chance.

When the '63 season ended, Tommy was once more called to

Birdie's office. "What are your plans for off-season?" the manager asked.

"I'm going back to college."

The older man shook his head. "We'd like you to go to Puerto Rico this winter." Ponce, Puerto Rico, was home for a winter baseball league that used aspiring ballplayers and gave others opportunities to work on problems—batting slumps, fielding basics, pitching difficulties, and so forth.

"We want you to work on the pick-off play, and get much-needed pitching experience, so you can be one of our starters in '64," explained Birdie.

John Lipon, manager of the Charleston team, also managed the Puerto Rico club. It was a good experience. Lipon knew Tommy's strengths and weaknesses, and the two could begin at once on building toward his first major league season.

After a few weeks of training, Tommy experienced a painful elbow injury. He went over to Lipon who ordered the trainers to ice it down. The next day the elbow was no better. It was as if the joint had somehow locked. Tommy could not raise his arm to feed himself, or make the simple twisting motion to open a doorknob.

Tommy went to a local Ponce doctor who diagnosed it as tendonitis and ordered two weeks of complete rest. The elbow slowly began to heal and only hurt when Tommy threw the ball at game speeds.

It was suggested that Tommy visit a specialist back in the States, so he flew to Saint Louis to see a Cardinal trainer, Bob Bauman, and a doctor recommended by another pitcher, Sonny Siebert.

Doctor I. C. Middleman, a Cardinal orthopedic specialist, was treating Tommy in his office when the news came from Dallas of President Kennedy's death. The tragedy quieted the two men temporarily. Finally, the doctor completed his diagnosis and treatment.

"You've torn some tendon fibers," explained Dr. Middleman. "This shot of cortisone will ease the pain."

Bauman met with Tommy and gave him a lead ball the size of a baseball. "I'm going to give you some exercises to do with this weighted ball. You do them all winter, and maybe you'll be ready to start next spring.''

On the way home, Tommy was lost in fearful thoughts. Perhaps the events of that day in Dallas triggered his thinking. It was his first real arm injury and the only thought racing through his troubled mind was *what if I never pitch again!* Imagine, so close to the dream and yet . . . .

Tommy made a conscious effort to dismiss such negative thinking and concentrate on the possibilities instead. It worked, along with the exercises and therapy given by Bob Bauman. By February, he reported to spring training and within two weeks of workouts was throwing the ball hard, and with no pain.

Tommy performed well for Cleveland during the spring-training exhibition games. Yet, because he was a rookie, he had to wait for the chance to "prove himself"—not only to his manager, but to his teammates as well. He was the sixth starting pitcher on a roster using only four starters. Consequently, during his first year in the majors, he was as stifled as he had been in Jacksonville when he wasn't even given a chance to pitch. He couldn't even wangle an opportunity to pitch in relief.

Tommy heard rumors that he was probably going to be sent back to the Portland, Oregon, farm club in the Pacific Coast League. Although major league clubs won't ship a player back down in the system without giving him a chance to "prove" himself with one game in the majors, he felt more like a sacrificial lamb. If he lost, Tommy knew he was out. He really had to demonstrate his ability if he was to stay. His opportunity came in a game against Baltimore, the second game of a doubleheader which assigned Tommy to pitch against the veteran ace (and Tommy's idol), Robin Roberts. In an amazing display of throwing ability, Tommy shut out the Orioles 3–0, on just 72 pitches and 3 hits for the 9 innings—a feat he himself has never been able to equal.

The game was important. American League umpire Joe Papperella said, "That's the greatest game I've ever seen pitched!" Suddenly Tommy was pitcher number five instead of last man. Reporters talked to him and treated him now like a major league pitcher. Pitching coach Early Wynn took an interest in Tommy.

"Son, you've got a good fast ball and nice curve ball. But I want you to learn to throw a slider," he said during batting practice one day.

Tommy studied the pitch, practiced it, and could throw it with only some ability. It was an easy pitch to throw for strikes and Tommy began to throw it to the exclusion of his other pitches. As he worked longer and longer on throwing a slider, Tommy found his confidence in his fast ball fading, forgetting the fast ball was his best pitch.

Birdie Tebbetts was recuperating from a heart attack in an Arizona hospital, so it fell on the shoulders of Gabe Paul, general manager of the Cleveland front office, to give Tommy his walking papers back down to Triple A ball.

"Seems like you've lost your pitching confidence, Tommy. Maybe you can find it again if we give you a regular assignment again. We're sending you to Portland. Your friend, Johnny Lipon, is managing the team. Lipon will let you pitch."

"You forgot how to pitch, T.J.," was the way John Lipon diagnosed the problem. "Forget all the advice people have been giving you about how to pitch, what pitches to throw, all that stuff. You've got a good fast ball, use it. Use your curve ball. *Forget* the slider! Forget everything else. Concentrate on pitching the pitches you do best."

After several weeks of pitching for the Portland club, the ability and confidence were restored. The self-assurance even rubbed off on Tommy's bat handle.

In a game against San Diego, a Cincinnati Red farm club, Tommy hit a grand-slam home run in the second inning. The next time at bat, he hit another homer—this time with two men on base. The third time at bat Tommy hit a long ball, again with the bases loaded, which the left fielder caught against the fence. It was an historic day—8 RBIs in a single game. Needless to say, Portland won.

Following that game, in a Labor Day doubleheader in Seattle, Portland was able to get two men on base and Tommy walked to the plate as a pinch hitter. Having heard of what happened in San Diego, the Seattle pitcher promptly gave Tommy an intentional walk, usually reserved for the top hitters when the pitcher is in a tight situation. Tommy laughed in hilarious disbelief, as he jogged down to first base.

Cleveland recalled Tommy at the end of the '64 season. They still didn't use him as a starter. Instead, though he was back in the "big leagues," it was for bull-pen relief pitching, usually only 1 or 2 innings every other day. He ended up with a 2–9 record.

At the end of the season, Tommy went back to Indiana State for more study. It was at home in Terre Haute that the news reached him in January.

"Tommy," his dad exclaimed, when he called him out of class, "we just heard from Gabe Paul. You've been traded!"

"T-traded? Who—where?"

"The White Sox. You'll be playing next year in Chicago."

3

With the White Sox

Tommy reported to the White Sox spring-training camp in Sarasota, Florida, with excitement at being picked by the second place team in the American League. He was included in General Manager Ed Short's welcome and introductory remarks which always started the new season.

Al Lopez, then the field manager, worked with Tommy to refine the basic elements of pitching. Lopez, probably the best defensive catcher in baseball history, could quickly spot pitching flaws and advise pitchers of their errors before they were ingrained as bad habits.

The White Sox did their best to help new ballplayers adjust. Yet, Tommy sensed something was still wrong. It was his pitching mechanics. The Sox management had nothing to compare it with, but Tommy knew something was not quite right. Sometimes he had the magic and his game was flawless. Other times he was way off. He was inconsistent and the problem was that Tommy didn't really know what to do about it.

The Sox management took note of Tommy's pitching and likewise sensed problems.

"You're rushing, T.J.," said pitching coach Ray Berres one day.

"What do you mean?" asked Tommy.

"Your mechanics are off. Concentrate on not rushing. Keep your elbow up. *Stay back.*"

Concentration didn't help. In fact, if anything it was like saying, "Think about what you're doing wrong and do it again, so you can see that it's wrong." Concentrating on something wrong, some slipped-in factor, was merely to reinforce it, not correct it.

Tommy tried to focus his thoughts and muscle "memories" on how he had done it before. It seemed to him, however, everything was the same.

One day, in a seemingly unrelated incident, Ray Berres came up to Tommy.

"T.J., you're quite a golfer. Come here and tell me what I'm doing wrong. I can't seem to hit the ball right."

"Sure," replied Tommy.

Ray had his clubs nearby and was hitting some wedge shots into the vacant outfield in Sarasota.

"There, you see—they never go straight," muttered Berres.

"Try it again while I watch," suggested Tommy.

Again Berres hit the ball and it careened into the grass some distance from where it was aimed.

"It's your swing, Ray," said Tommy. "Take your club back nice and easy. Feel when it's right. Then swing—reverse the motion, nice and easy—then boom! You hit the ball, and follow through. You're rushing into the swing too soon and it's throwing you off."

Now both men knew that what Ray was doing with his wedge shot was exactly what Tommy was doing in his pitching motion.

"You're rushing your motion—take it nice and easy," repeated Ray. "Let's both try it." Ray raised the club smoothly and swung it just as gracefully. The clubhead smacked the ball and lifted it with a high arcing trajectory, just as it was supposed to.

"Now," Berres said, "let's see what happens when you try it."

When Tommy got to the pitching mound it was obvious to them all that the problem had been located. Now his concentration could lock on to the mechanics of the motion and not whatever he thought he was doing wrong.

Tommy was learning about pitching all over again. It was exciting and he really enjoyed playing for Chicago. In the 1965 season Tommy was the White Sox's most effective starter. Not a bad year for a pitcher who had trouble with the mechanics in spring training. At the end of his first season with the Sox, he was called into the manager's office.

"Tommy, congratulations on a fine season. Your 14–7 record is a good one—and the 21 consecutive scoreless innings was a great 3 games. Well, we're happy at the way you're progressing."

"Thank you, sir."

"How's the arm—any problems since last winter?"

"No, Al, I think Bob Bauman and Doctor Middleman took care of it pretty well," Tommy responded to Lopez's question.

"Listen, we want you to spend some time in Puerto Rico this winter. As you know, Charlie Metro coaches our team down there. We'd like you to work on your pick-off move to first base—it's a little tougher for a left-handed pitcher—and maybe it'll help your game." Puerto Rico baseball also gave the young player an extra season of pitching in the same calendar year.

Tommy followed their advice and played baseball until Christmas break. Then he went home to rest until February when spring training started again.

That winter the White Sox organization was shaken up. Manager Al Lopez resigned and a controversial new leader had been hired to pilot the team.

Eddie Stanky was introduced to the media at a press conference in Chicago. Until that time, Tommy had never met him either. The talk was that Eddie ran a tight ship and quite a few ballplayers didn't care for him. What the new season would bring was anyone's guess.

As a "clean-cut" young idol of youngsters, Tommy was often asked to speak, or share his Christian faith in churches, schools, or for civic groups. Often, he was asked to speak at sports functions. At once such event, later that winter, Tommy found himself appearing with Eddie Stanky at a sports banquet in Rockford, Illinois. The ninety-minute drive over to Rockford from Chicago gave the two men a chance to become better acquainted.

"Do you work out in the off-season, young man?"

"Yes, I do, as a matter of fact," replied Tommy.

"Good. I believe in physical conditioning."

The car moved along steadily and another lull in the conversation prompted a follow-up question.

"Where do you work out—what do you do?"

"Well, I work out at Indiana State with the football and basketball players. Weights . . . that kind of thing. You know . . . ."

"Uh-huh."

"And I usually run maybe three miles a day."

"Good. I believe in physical conditioning," Eddie repeated.

On the way back to Chicago, the new manager proved that he knew more about Tommy than Tommy knew of his new boss. They discussed Tommy's history as a ballplayer, his mistakes and triumphs, and what he had learned. Tommy filled in the gaps and his answers seemed to satisfy Eddie.

"Young man," Stanky said finally, "how good a fielder are you?"

"Fair," Tommy admitted.

"Can you bunt . . . hit and run?"

"Uh . . . yes . . . sometimes," Tommy replied. It wasn't the answer Stanky wanted, but he knew it was honest. He nodded.

"I know. Listen . . . do me two things in spring training—work as hard as you can on fielding and hitting . . . ."

"And the second thing?"

"Your curve ball. I want you to use it 70 percent of the time in spring-training games. Every ten pitches you throw, make seven of them curves. Okay?"

"Yes sir. Sounds fair enough."

Stanky knew that this spring-training practice would give Tommy an edge by the time the season started. When the game "counted," Tommy would be able to throw a curve-ball strike to a batter with a 3–2 count and the bases loaded.

"You know, young man," Eddie paused to choose his next words carefully," I believe you are going to be one of the best pitchers in baseball! I believe in you."

There was excellent rapport between these two men after that. Whatever problems others may have had with Eddie Stanky, they never arose with Tommy and Eddie.

He finished the 1966 season with a 14–11 record and went home to remark to his dad, "I learned more about baseball under Eddie Stanky than I did the rest of my life all together!"

In 1966, Tommy was forced to make a decision which, if left undecided, would affect his baseball career profoundly. Three days before being drafted into the army for at least two years away from baseball, Tommy decided to enlist in the Indiana Air National Guard and fulfull his military obligation without interrupting his career. The enlistment required two weeks of summer camp and active duty drills which could be scheduled around the playing season.

Tommy reported to Hulman Field in Terre Haute, for his annual training, after completing basic training at Lackland Air Force Base in San Antonio, Texas. In basic training sessions he was taught how to fire a weapon on the rifle range. However, for his duty, he was assigned the task of typing, filing and other clerical chores.

In 1967, with the worry of the draft behind him, Tommy could now concentrate on another good season with the White Sox. And it was an outstanding year. Five of his first eight wins were shutouts. By the All-Star Game break in July, Tommy already had an impressive 8–5 record. He was one of the spark plugs that put Eddie Stanky's Sox in first place, but was not included on the All-Star team.

Then, suddenly, Tommy became ill with what he at first thought was a common flu virus. But the "bug" hung on. Tommy got worse, his weight dropped from 192 to 170 in just 10 days. He was unable to eat solid foods and diarrhea dehydrated his body and left him weak. He was only able to keep cold liquids down, so his diet consisted of Cokes, lemonade, punch, milk, and bananas.

During this time, Tommy was scheduled to report for two weeks of active duty. Since the Air National Guard had relieved him of duty on weekends, the Sox had scheduled him to pitch in Kansas City on Sunday.

Tommy was in summer camp, ill, and couldn't perform his reserve duty efficiently but took a chance that he'd feel better by game time Sunday. He flew to Kansas City and suited up, but didn't work out.

Only when Tommy began to pitch did the seriousness of his illness become apparent. He started the inning and pitched to the first few batters. Suddenly he got dizzy and couldn't maintain his equilibrium.

From the sidelines Eddie Stanky signaled "Time out" to the umpire and rushed to the mound. Two White Sox players also ran over.

"What's the matter, T.J.?" asked Eddie.

"I'm sick . . . help me to the dugout. I'm dizzy . . . ."

The game was stopped as Tommy staggered toward the bench, supported on the arms of his teammates.

The trainer rushed up to assist Tommy's teammates in laying him on a bench. Then he took a cold towel drenched with ammonia and applied it to his head and face to keep Tommy from passing out.

Eddie Stanky called the bull pen and ordered another pitcher in the game, then turned to see how Tommy was doing.

The team put him on a plane to Chicago with instructions to check into a hospital. Tommy was hospitalized for several days of tests while doctors tried to find the cause of his mysterious illness. Acquaintances and well-wishers sent their best. Friends from the Fellowship of Christian Athletes, in which Tommy held membership, sent word of their prayers for his recovery. There was plenty of time to think and pray about his condition. He knew of another athlete with similar symptoms who steadily weakened. It turned out that he had contracted some form of virulent cancer. The thought sent a shiver through Tommy in spite of the July heat.

"If it was something simple like flu or some virus, they'd have learned it by now and told me," mused Tommy as he prepared himself for really bad news. Yet, though the tests were done by the hospital personnel, no one was able to give any concrete information.

"The fact is," said Tommy's doctor, "you've been here four days and we can't find out what you've got."

"Terrific," muttered Tommy.

"Well, let me brighten the picture," the doctor continued. "We've ruled out the really bad stuff—hepatitis, leukemia, mono, blood disease, tumors, nerves. We think you've got some mysterious virus."

"When will I get over it?"

The doctor shrugged. "I don't know. But it's up to you—you can stay here in Chicago and recover, or go home and rest."

"That's an easy choice," Tommy grinned. "I can lie in bed just as easy in Terre Haute as Chicago."

"Just make sure that you do," warned the doctor. "Complete bed rest for several weeks is the only way to lick this thing."

For the rest of July and part of August, Tommy rested in Terre

Haute. He recovered enough so that the diarrhea stopped and he could finally eat solid foods again, but he couldn't put his weight back on. Tommy's mom cooked lots of potatoes, spaghetti, casseroles, and foods designed to do the trick. But the only ones who gained weight were . . . his parents!

Tommy reported back to the ball club in the middle of August and tried to pick up where he had left off. But the sizzle that went into the 8–5 record earlier was gone with his strength. He won only 2 more games the whole season. One of the two wins was a masterful win over the Boston Red Sox in Fenway Park—a graveyard for left-handed pitchers. Tommy shut out the Red Sox 5–0 (the Red Sox played in the World Series against the Yankees that year). The amazing feat in this game was the 23 ground-ball outs recorded that afternoon. Manager Eddie Stanky gave any White Sox pitcher to get at least 20 ground balls in a 9-inning win a new suit of clothes. When the club got back to Chicago, Tommy went out to the best clothing store in Chicago and bought a new suit and sent Manager Stanky the bill for five hundred dollars.

Between the 1967–68 seasons, Tommy tried to get back in shape. He spent most of the winter playing golf in various baseball and celebrity Pro-Am tournaments. He finally did put the weight back on by spring training. However, 1968 started out badly for the White Sox, yet good for Tommy. The team lost its first 10 games of the season. Tommy was fortunate in those 10 games not to suffer a loss. He broke the losing streak by beating the Minnesota Twins 3–2. Tommy was 7–0 with 1 shutout by the All-Star break, and his earned-run-average was 1.68, the best it had ever been in his major league career. Tommy's superb record enabled him to be picked as one of eight pitchers for the American League in the All-Star Game which was played in Houston that year, 1968.

However, Tommy's fortunes turned sour along with those of the White Sox after that. In the muggy heat of the August 22 evening, Tommy was pitching in Detroit. After 3 innings, he had a count of 3 balls and 2 strikes on the Detroit batter, Dick McAuliffe. The next pitch was almost wild, and went over the batter's head for a ball 4—and a walk. But the batter apparently thought Tommy had thrown the ball at him intentionally and came charging out to the mound, throwing his bat away.

Tommy knew by the look in McAuliffe's eyes that he was going to start punching away. Tommy reasoned that rather than catching any swinging punches, it would be better to meet Dick head-on, wrestle him to the ground, and hold on until the umpires or players could separate them and the flaring tempers could cool. However, before he could do this, McAuliffe was already there. His knee struck Tommy's left shoulder and his momentum drove him right over the pitcher, pretty much the way an unsuspecting safety in football might be run over by a mountain of a halfback.

When the two men were finally pulled apart, it was too late. Tommy was badly injured. His left (pitching arm) shoulder had been separated and he was forced to leave the game. Two shoulder ligaments were torn and the injury knocked Tommy out of action as a pitcher for the rest of '68, with his record of 10–5. Tommy's good friend, former All-Pro middle linebacker Bill George of the Los Angeles Rams phoned and offered to give Tommy tackling lessons in the off-season.

The White Sox team doctor suggested surgery to mend the torn shoulder, but Tommy was hesitant, wondering if the injury couldn't heal without an operation. For a pitcher an operation in his pitching arm could mean an early retirement. He consulted Dr. Danny Levinthal, a noted orthopedist in the Chicago and Los Angeles areas, a friend, who advised against surgery. Tommy's attorney, Bill Sampson, also voted against an operation so Tommy decided to wait it out.

Tommy went to Sarasota, Florida, in October and November to pitch for the White Sox Instructional League team. He didn't get into any games, but went through all the rigors of training to test the injured arm. The arm responded to the rest and was going to be ready for the 1969 season with the White Sox.

Meanwhile, the Sox continued their downhill slide, and decided to fire manager Eddie Stanky. Tommy was saddened at this news but had learned to expect things like this in the game of baseball.

The one thing that made the year a little better was Tommy's meeting, later that year, the girl who was to become his wife.

4

Sally Simmons

Sally Simmons was a nineteen-year-old Indiana State University coed. She had been especially selected to be one of the school's Blue Berets, an elite group of student hosts and hostesses which served the University president's office.

It was Homecoming Week in October, and the usual fifteen thousand student population was increased by thousands of alumni who also crowded the campus. All were looking forward with excitement to the game. Sally's responsibility this day was to escort the father of Senator Birch Bayh to the "Distinguished Alumni" ceremony of the weekend.

While escorting the honored alumnus to the field at half time, Sally glanced across the sidelines to where a tall, good-looking man was standing. She didn't recall seeing him on campus before, and assumed he was with the news media.

Sally was impressed by his clothes, which showed good taste and style—except for the shoes. He was wearing a bright yellow turtleneck and contrasting checked sports coat. But his shoes were white.

That's unusual, she thought to herself, *why would anyone wear white shoes in October?* She didn't know, of course, he'd just flown in from a golf vacation in the Bahamas.

Just then the young man saw her. Their eyes met for an instant and Sally blushed. She quickly averted her eyes and moved on to the field.

Tommy, meanwhile, standing at the sidelines, was watching the festivities before leaving for California for more rest and golf between baseball seasons. He noticed one of the girls on the field. Their gaze met and he smiled. She looked away shyly.

Tommy turned to his friend, John Knox, who was the reason Tommy was present. John was captain of the football team and Tommy was anxious to see his friend play.

"Hey, John, do you know that girl?"

"Which one?" John asked.

"The one over there," Tommy replied, "the one who's dressed like an airline stewardess."

"Sure. She's a friend of mine—Sally Simmons." Then John added with a smile, "You have good taste, T.J. She's a finalist in the ISU beauty pageant—a Plainfield Junior Miss in the Indiana Junior Miss pageant . . . a real doll! Would you like to meet her?"

A week later John Knox saw Sally walking across campus and called out to her. She waited for him.

"Did you ever hear of Tommy John?" he asked.

"No . . . I don't think so. Should I?"

"He's a pitcher for the White Sox," John explained.

"I've never heard of them either."

This is going to be slow, John thought.

"It's a Chicago baseball team. Anyway," he continued, "Tommy John is from Terre Haute and a good friend of mine. Would you be interested in going out with him?"

Although she considered herself to have led a pretty sheltered life in Plainfield, Indiana (population 5,000), Sally was sophisticated enough to have heard some of the rumors about "girl chasing" professional ballplayers.

"No, *thanks!*" she said curtly, then added, "I'm sure your friend will have no trouble getting a date. Besides, he's too old for me."

"Old? He's just twenty-four!"

"And I'm only nineteen. That's too much difference," Sally said, closing the discussion. "He's as old as my sister, Judy, and she's married."

Knox shrugged, strode off, and later gave the bad news to his friend.

"Looks like we struck out, badly," he told Tommy. "She won't go out with ballplayers."

That winter, Indiana State was playing a basketball game with Ball State University. Sally, an ISU cheerleader, had sprained her ankle so badly she had to hobble around for a while. Her date for the basketball game, a fellow student, helped her climb up into the bleachers.

From her vantage point, she saw a visitor watching the game from the sidelines. She recognized the good-looking man with white shoes she had seen at Homecoming. This time, however, he wasn't wearing white shoes. She wondered who he was.

Then someone else caught her eye. Standing nearby was John Knox, an usher for the game. He had been talking to the good-looking man in the black trench coat. She watched John Knox looking through the audience for someone. When he saw Sally, his eyes lit up.

Across the crowded gym, Knox yelled out her name. "Sally . . . Sally Simmons. Hey, Simmons, come on down here! I want you to meet Tommy John!"

Sally was convinced the game itself had stopped and the entire audience had hushed to look at her. She felt her face turn hot and crimson. Her date nudged her gently and whispered, "What's that all about?"

"I don't *know*," Sally replied.

"Hey, Simmons—here's Tommy John! Come here!" came the booming voice from the floor. Up in the bleachers Sally was too mortified to even look up. Her date was embarrassed and looked sharply at John Knox. Meanwhile, Tommy—also red with embarrassment—was tugging at John and repeating, "No, John . . . that's okay, John. Some other time . . . John . . . not now." Finally Tommy's tugs got stronger and John relented.

It was several minutes before Sally's embarrassment would allow her to look up again. When she did, John Knox and the handsome man in the trench coat were gone. "So *that's* Tommy John," she thought.

Some days later Sally was caring for an assignment, one of her duties in the Blue Berets. Doctor Alan C. Rankin, president of Indiana State University, walked up and chatted briefly. Doctor Rankin was a personable administrator who knew his students and showed personal interest in their problems and needs. In fact, Sally did not realize just how much Dr. Rankin *did* know about his students.

"Sally, what's this I hear about you not wanting to go out with Tommy John?"

"Who . . . I mean . . . how did you . . . ?" Sally stammered.

Doctor Rankin chuckled, "One of your friends mentioned it to me, because I'm a friend of Tommy's."

"Oo-oh, that John Knox—I'll wring his neck!"

Doctor Rankin laughed. "John means well, it's just that he's a better football player than Cupid. I only mention it because—well, I know the kind of girl you are, and wanted to say you don't have to be afraid of going out with Tommy. He's a nice young man who holds the same values as you do. Tommy has my stamp of approval, if that means anything."

Sally smiled. "At first I didn't know who he was, or anything about him. But after seeing him, and after hearing so many people plead his case, how can I *not* go out with him?"

The two of them laughed and the incident was forgotten—until Saturday morning when the phone in Sally's dorm rang.

"Sally Simmons! Telephone," D.J., Sally's friend yelled.

Sally came to the phone in her pajamas and hair up in curlers.

"Hello," she yawned.

"Sally? Sally Simmons?" the voice asked.

"Yes. Who is this?"

"Sally . . . this is Tommy John. I just wanted to apologize for what happened at the game the other day."

Sally looked at the receiver and frowned. "Who is this—really? John Knox, is that you?"

"No . . . Sally. It's Tommy John."

"John Knox, is this another one of your jokes?"

"It's not a joke, Sally. I'm wondering if you'll go out with me?"

Sally sat there without answering. It really *was* Tommy John. Now the embarrassment that reddened her face at the game returned. "Oh, I'm sorry . . . I thought you were John Knox playing a joke."

"But, *will* you? Go out with me, I mean?"

"Yes . . . I guess so. When?"

"This morning. How about if I pick you up in twenty minutes and we go out for coffee?"

Twenty minutes! Sally panicked. It was about 8:15 in the morning and she'd just gotten up. She cradled the receiver back on the telephone and whimpered a quick *help!* Then she ran back to her room to dress and get ready. In the rush to get prepared, she had not remembered that she didn't even like coffee.

Exactly twenty minutes later Tommy pulled up in front of the dorm. By then the word was out. Sally asked a roommate to greet him and have him wait "just a second" in the lobby. As he waited, there was a lively procession of coeds who "just happened" to pass through on some kind of business or another. On a second floor landing, several of her Chi Omega sorority sisters watched and appraised him.

"He's handsome."

"And tall."

"Look at those clothes. The guys around here don't wear clothes like that."

"He must have girls in every city the team goes to."

"Boy, if Sally doesn't want him, I'm available."

"I wonder if I could get an autograph . . . for my brother, of course."

In a few moments Sally came down. Tommy courteously greeted her, opened the door politely, and helped her into the car. As they drove along, Sally found her first impressions of Tommy John were good ones. She liked his manners and soft-spoken conversation. He was asking questions about her and joking about how "with friends like John Knox, who needs enemies?"

He pulled the car into the parking lot of a local Big Wheel restaurant and helped her with the door again.

When the waitress came to take their order, Tommy said, "Two coffees?" questioning Sally. Rather than appear unsophisticated and admitting she didn't drink coffee, Sally nodded.

"Tell me about yourself," Tommy prompted. Shyly at first, Sally answered his questions, then before long the initial tension was broken and they laughed and talked easily.

When the waitress brought the coffee, Sally couldn't admit she'd never tasted the stuff before and ask how to use cream or sugar. She watched Tommy for a clue, but he drank his coffee black. She lifted the cup to her lips and sipped. It was a hot, bitter brew. Her taste buds argued with her, but she took another sip.

During the conversation she had somehow drunk the entire cup. Also, she learned about Tommy, a little about baseball—that he was now in his off-season (and what that meant). She began to like this good-looking man. He was not the typical stereotype of the bragging "jock." Instead, the talk drew her out, and opened her up to his friendliness and charm. By the time they finished, he had gotten her not only to try coffee but accept a date with him for the following night.

Their date consisted of her accompanying him to nearby Worthington, Indiana, where Tommy was scheduled to speak at a local Little League sports banquet.

"It's a banquet, so we'll eat there," he had told her. They were both quite hungry by the time they reached Worthington only to learn there had been a misunderstanding—it would be the first banquet they attended where food was not served!

They made the best of the situation, however, and Tommy joked about it when it came time for him to speak. During his talk, Sally learned even more about him—both by what he said and how he said it. His counsel to aspiring youngsters was well received. He talked about his religious and patriotic convictions without embarrassment. Following the speech, youngsters crowded around Tommy for autographs. He patiently obliged each one.

After every one left, Tommy and Sally got their coats and started for the parking lot and Tommy's car.

They joked about the misunderstanding of a banquet without food as they pulled away and drove back toward the college. After driving for some time, Tommy made a comment about how late it was getting. Then he pulled the car off the highway and into a parking lot. Sally noticed the sign out front and caught her breath—ALBERT PICK MOTEL—with its VACANCY sign flashing on and off. She panicked. *Then it's true about baseball players and their girl friends,* she said to herself.

Tommy interrupted her thoughts. "We'll stop and eat at their coffee shop before going back."

Sally was both chagrined and relieved—and upset with herself for doubting Tommy's character and integrity. After a late sandwich snack, they were on their way again so Tommy could bring Sally back to the dorm before curfew.

After that they began to date more frequently, although they seldom did anything special. In fact, many dates were enjoyable visits to Tommy's parents' house for dinner and an evening of watching TV. Sally listened happily for hours as Tommy's dad entertained her with his stories, especially those about his son's childhood. Other times Sally brought her books along to study. When she and Tommy went out, it was often to a movie or campus show, or a college game. Sometimes they joined Tommy's friend Bob McClelland for dinner. When Tommy left for spring training, Sally tried to evaluate her thoughts and emotions. It was still too early to have any specific serious thoughts, but one thing was certain. She was glad she had decided to go out with the friend of John Knox who played professional baseball.

At nine years old, Tommy John had already shown his love for baseball. *Below:* Tommy's team won the Little League Championships. His dad (far right, second row) was the manager. Young Tommy is in the second row, fifth from left. (Photo by Leo Deming Studio)

Tommy John was an excellent basketball player, too. He is shown here with one of the all-time coaching greats, Adolph Rupp of the University of Kentucky. (Lexington Herald-Leader Staff Photo)

In 1958 Tommy's baseball team won the Indiana State Babe Ruth Championship. Again his father was his coach. Mr. John, Sr., is standing second row, far right. Tommy is in the second row, second from left. *Below:* Meanwhile, in Plainfield, Indiana, Sally Simmons was growing up. Here she is with her kindergarten class, second row, fourth from the left. (Maple Hill Studio, Plainfield, Indiana)

Sally was a cheerleader at Plainfield High School, far left. (Photo by Frederick Barker Studio) *Left:* After Tommy John, Jr., was graduated from Gerstmeyer High School in Terre Haute, Indiana, he was signed by the Cleveland Indian organization. This was taken at Tucson, Arizona, in 1962.

Tommy was traded to the Chicago White Sox. At Comiskey Park in 1966, Tommy (third from left) is shown with the Sox pitching staff. (Photo by John Jaqua) *Left:* Tommy had joined the Indiana Air National Guard.

The young pitcher met and courted Sally Simmons at Indiana State University. They were married on July 13, 1970. Left to right: Mr. and Mrs. Simmons, Sally, Tommy, and Tommy's parents, Mr. and Mrs. Tommy John, Sr. (Photo by Bob Harvey) *Left:* Tommy, recovering from arm surgery, visits Sally in Saint Jude's Hospital after the birth of Tami, September 1974.

His arm in a cast, Tommy feeds two-week-old Tami. *Below:* This scoreboard speaks for itself. Tommy, recuperating from extremely serious surgery, threw out the first ball in the play-offs in 1974.

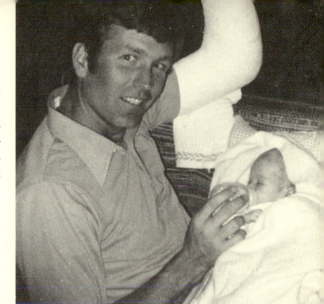

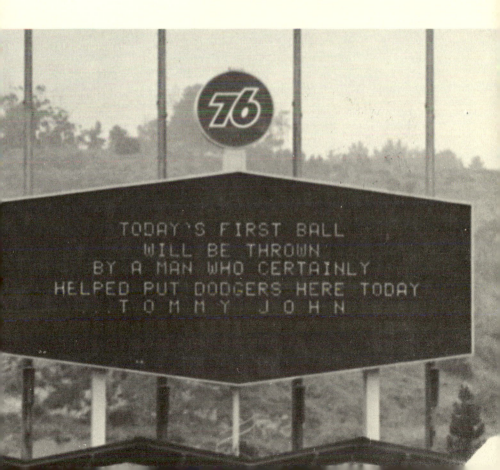

TODAY'S FIRST BALL
WILL BE THROWN
BY A MAN WHO CERTAINLY
HELPED PUT DODGERS HERE TODAY
TOMMY JOHN

5

Courtship

A baseball players' strike delayed the start of spring training in 1969. It also gave Tommy and Sally more time to spend with each other, getting to know one another. Tommy finally left in March for Sarasota. Neither of them had given the other any indication that their relationship was serious. Sally felt she wanted to get to know Tommy better, to learn about his life and work, to spend some time alone just thinking. She dated guys at college, but mostly for social reasons. None of them really measured up to Tommy when she compared them.

Tommy's thoughts were also in a jumble. He knew the widely told rumors about baseball players having a girl in every town they played. But he knew it was a misconception, particularly in his own situation.

Some people on the club thought he must be a bit strange—after all, he was twenty-seven and single. His dates were mainly social, too. He dated stewardesses, TV personalities, models, girls he met while golfing or at church. But he was so wrapped up in baseball and golf that he'd never thought seriously about marriage. As a matter of fact, even now as he thought about it, the idea almost frightened him.

But he continued to correspond with Sally and phone her regularly—and missing their times together.

He began to concentrate on his playing baseball now. There were two obstacles to care for before his mind could deal with the '69 season. The first one was his contract. Because of his shoulder injury and Tommy's lack of action in 1968, the White Sox were reluctant to grant him an increase in his salary. In fact, the management (with his manager and friend, Eddie Stanky, gone) was even having second thoughts about Tommy's continuing in the majors.

Tommy consulted his attorney, Bill Sampson, about talking to the White Sox management.

"Listen," Bill offered, "let's make Tommy's increase contingent on pitching 200 innings. He'll only be able to do that if he stays in the game—and he'll only stay in if he's pitching well."

The White Sox agreed, so the first mental obstacle was behind Tommy. The second block was going to take more than positive thinking to overcome. The Sox installed Astroturf at Comiskey Park. Tommy and others on the team who had to pitch on the lightning-fast new vinyl grass believed the Astroturf was a mistake. The reason for Tommy's apprehension over the Astroturf was due to the fact that Tommy, a sinker-ball specialist and always throwing a lot of ground balls, would be giving up a lot of ground-ball base hits and consequently more base runners. More base runners meant possibly more runs scored against the pitcher. The White Sox had not improved their offense that much and the odds for a good season were slim. But he would be willing to try his best when the season opened.

During spring training at Sarasota, Tommy arranged things with his good friend Bob McClelland, who owned an auto dealership in Terre Haute, to provide Sally and a few friends from ISU with a car to drive to Florida during Easter break, with the condition that they drive to Sarasota to see Tommy. The girls drove to Daytona Beach or Miami in other years for a few days of sun and excitement. With a little persuasion, this year they drove to Sarasota instead. Tommy saw Sally after workouts and they had time for some fun and relaxation before it was time for the girls to drive back to Indiana State.

Sally and Tommy saw each other very seldom during the season. They would make a point of getting together on weekends when he had reserve meetings in his hometown, allowing them to have dinner on Saturday nights.

In June, Tommy arranged for Sally to accompany his parents for a

road trip to Anaheim, Oakland, and Seattle, where the White Sox
were playing. She stayed at the hotel with his parents, visited him at
the game, and went sightseeing as a foursome during the day.

Tommy had never met a girl with the qualities and values that
Sally had. Just being together was fun. At a time when many young
people were rejecting traditional moral attitudes, Tommy was comfortable with this girl who shared his ideas, Christian experience,
and goals. The idea of marriage was less threatening to him now that
he could see so much that was worthwhile in Sally. He also appreciated her personality and down-to-earth behavior. He was always
proud to take her out with him—she knew how to dress, how to use
makeup, how to act with grace and poise—plus she was an intelli-
gent conversationalist. If he had made a list of all the good qualities
he wanted in a girl, he could not find them all in one girl as he already
had with Sally. Still, he had not discussed his ideas with her or
anyone else. He was too busy concentrating on his baseball game.

A positive attitude did not help Tommy with his problems with
Astroturf. As the season slipped by, Tommy's record did also. Before his injury the previous year, his record was 10–5 with a 1.98
ERA; this year, he ended the season 9–11 with a 3.25 ERA. He did
well enough to pitch 232 innings, though, and earned his salary
increase from the White Sox.

In September, Sally had started her senior year at ISU. Her major
was physical education, and she began to wonder if she should
teach, or find something else for a career, or place to use her talents
until—her mind toyed with the word—*marriage*.

Tommy helped with the first part of the decision when he recommended her to a Terre Haute TV station. The general manager of
WTHI–TV, Paul Denehie, a friend of Tommy's, was having dinner
with Tommy and Sally one evening.

"Sally," Paul asked during a conversational lull, "how'd you like
to be on TV?"

"Me? What would *I* do?"

"Well, we have this kids' show—it's called 'Dr. Hopp's Animal
Show.' Dr. Hopp is a zoologist from ISU—maybe you know him.
Anyway, what we need is an on-camera assistant for Dr. Hopp. It's

only a half-hour show, and it's taped—so you can work it around your classes. What do you say?"

"Sure . . . I'll give it a try. It sounds like fun."

It proved to be an understatement, for Sally loved animals—and on "Dr. Hopp's Animal Show"—that's what they had in abundance.

It took a great deal of convincing to reassure Tommy, when he later visited the studio during a TV taping, that the six-foot-long boa constrictor wrapped around Sally was harmless!

From this initial start, Sally worked into other jobs at the station in the promotion department. She wrote ten-second spots to promote reruns of "Beverly Hillbillies" and "That Girl" being aired afternoons by WTHI–TV. However, in spite of the work assigned her, it became routine and boring. She tried getting some assignments that were a little more creative. She worked out copy and ideas for a jacket commercial which she and Tommy videotaped. It was very effective for the local Root's Department Store (in addition to winning an advertising award).

With her self-confidence thus bolstered, she worked on other commercials; then one day she decided she'd like to sell time to sponsors.

"Girls don't sell advertising," was the sales manager's reply. It was said with a smile, but Bob Larr no doubt meant it.

"That's because no girl has ever been given the chance," Sally responded. "Bob, you've been the one guy here at the station who's helped me the most. All I know about TV and broadcasting I learned from you. It's exciting and I wish now my major was communications instead of education. But, Bob, you've got to let me try and sell advertising."

Bob seemed adamant. It was station policy.

"But what if I could land an account no one else could get—would you let me sell them?"

"Like who?" Bob asked.

Sally thought fast. Tommy's car-dealer friend Bob McClelland had been approached by the station, but he always turned them down. Sally knew the reason he turned down the spots and also

knew she and Tommy could probably persuade him to spend some
of his advertising budget at WTHI–TV, since he was already on
other local TV stations.

"How about if I land a contract with Terre Haute Chrysler-
Plymouth?" Sally asked.

Bob Larr raised his eyebrows, then his eyes twinkled. He had
been trying to land that one for some time, and if any account was
impossible, it was this one.

"Sure, if you sell Terre Haute Chrysler-Plymouth, you've got a
job in sales," Bob consented.

Sally walked back to her desk and called the car dealer. McClelland chuckled over her approach and said, "Sure, put me down for
two thousand dollars worth of TV."

In less than five minutes Sally was back in Bob Larr's office,
asking for a sales contract. His mouth dropped open, then he
laughed and said, "Welcome to the Sales Department."

Bob assigned her to a veteran salesman, Dick Forbes. She went
with Dick on calls, watched him at work with clients and made an
effort to learn as much as she could. She responded to the challenge
of selling. The station gave her accounts the other salesmen were
unable to land, and she won many of them.

Tommy came for Homecoming at ISU at Sally's request. It was
her senior year and the event would hold special sentimental meaning. Tommy wasn't all that impressed by the college traditions, but
went—basically to please Sally. He also went to see Johnny Carson,
who made a personal appearance at the university for the occasion.

Sally thought Tommy's indifference to Homecoming was a way of
putting her down. She wondered how serious Tommy was in his
feelings for her. He had expressed affection for her, phoned her,
wrote, and otherwise showed he cared—that he was serious. But
serious enough for marriage? And what about her own feelings? Did
she love *him?* She discussed her thoughts with a close girl friend,
Karen Barlow. The two girls made tentative plans to spend a year in
Europe and take time to sift through their thoughts and ideas of the
future. Also, Sally loved her TV job and was moving up the ladder.

She couldn't evaluate Tommy's seriousness because of a physical relationship. They both shared the often-ridiculed idea that sex belonged in marriage, so Tommy had never taken advantage of her.

Sally knew that Tommy was shy, but she was not forward either. She wondered if she or Tommy could ever get to the place where they could muster the courage to tell one another how much they cared, and their thoughts about a future together.

Two weeks before Christmas, Tommy came by to pick up Sally. They planned another of their dinner-TV-studying dates at Tommy's parents' home.

Sally dashed through the blustery night wind and was almost out of breath when she got inside the car. She settled back and expected Tommy to pull away from the dorm. Instead he turned on the inside dome light, grinned, and handed her a small package.

She blinked and opened the tiny box. Inside was a beautiful diamond engagement ring. She looked at it, awestruck, then hugged Tommy.

"W-w-will you m-m-marry m-me?" he stammered.

"Of course I will," Sally exclaimed, throwing her arms around him. Tommy kissed her and they drove off.

After dinner, Sally could not confine her jubilation.

"Could we drive to Plainfield and tell my folks?" she asked him.

"Sure . . . but it'll be late when we get back—it's sixty miles each way."

It was an exciting reunion. Sally's folks had gotten to know Tommy and were happy for their daughter.

The couple found it easier and easier to communicate—to share serious ideas with each other. They planned for an October wedding, following the baseball season and Tommy's fall Guard duty.

6

Love and Marriage—and Baseball

There was another change in White Sox managers in 1970. Al Lopez, who was field manager when Tommy had joined the club, replaced Eddie Stanky after Eddie was sacked in 1968. Lopez managed the team for part of the 1969 season, and Don Gutteridge was hired to take Lopez's place when illness forced Lopez to retire before the season ended. Gutteridge was retained for the 1970 season as well.

One wisecrack making the rounds said the White Sox had more managers than fans. White Sox third base coach Tony Cuccinello actually counted the attendance one night at Comiskey Park. He missed the actual count by just thirty people. "They were probably down buying a hot dog" he laughed. Morale in the club had sagged terribly during those couple of years and with it so did the performance of the team. The team lost 106 games—the worst record in the major leagues.

Tommy was a "veteran" on the White Sox team and pitched every fourth game. He pitched every fourth day regardless of what happened between days. If he pitched on Monday and games were rained out on Tuesday, Wednesday, and Thursday, he was scheduled to pitch Friday, skipping over the other pitchers. This select treatment is usually reserved for the pitcher in whom the manager has the most confidence. He won a trophy-clock inscribed THE FAVORITE WHITE SOX PLAYER, indicating he was also popular with the loyal fans, who kept coming out in spite of the team's overall performance.

In addition to the front-office changes, the players themselves just weren't meshing properly. It was a young club with many fresh ballplayers up from the minor leagues, who didn't seem to have the training they needed to play effectively in the major leagues.

It became apparent as early as spring training that the club was going to have one of the worst teams in the league that year.

Sally and her friends, who were graduating from ISU in June, drove down again at Easter with another McClelland car. They stopped at Sarasota where the Sox were training. She and Tommy decided to move their wedding date up from October in order for Tommy to be able to head immediately for California for Air Guard duty after the season.

"We'll get married at All-Star break in July, and you can go on the road with me for a couple of trips," Tommy said.

On July 13, Tommy and Sally were married at the Plainfield United Methodist Church. It was a big event in Plainfield—the Simmonses were a popular, well-respected family among the 5,000 residents. Friends and family members drove in from all parts of the area. Teammates came down from Chicago in a convoy of rented cars. The local gas-station operator on the main highway did his best day of business ever. Between wipes on windshields, the attendant even anticipated the questions.

"Excuse me, can you tell me . . . ?"

"The Methodist church is two blocks east and a block south. The Simmons live that way—just take the highway and turn left at the light."

The wedding was to be at 7:30 P.M., so while Sally, her sorority sisters, and family nervously waited and dressed, Tommy made use of the time during the day to play in a local golf tournament!

By evening guests were packed into the Plainfield Methodist Church. The air conditioning had broken down, and Sally wished the ceremony was over so the people would not become restless and uncomfortable.

Tommy's sister, Marilyn Hyde, sang before Sally and her father walked down the aisle. As the music played in the background, Sally looked at the front of the church where Tommy was waiting for her. He was smiling, his eyes sparkling with appreciation for this moment. Tommy had asked his dad to be best man; Sally had asked her sister to be her matron of honor. It was a meaningful time to be shared with their loved ones.

"I now pronounce you man and wife," the minister said. "You may kiss the bride."

Tommy lifted the filmy veil and tenderly kissed the new Mrs. Thomas Edward John, Jr., whom the minister had just introduced.

The organ began the wedding recessional, and the two of them started down the aisle. However, Sally stopped when she came to where her mother was seated. She reached down to embrace her.

"Oh, Mom—I love you!" Sally cried.

Mrs. Simmons hugged her daughter, her own eyes filling.

"Oh, Mom," Sally whispered, "I love Tommy so much—but . . . I don't want to leave you and Daddy."

Mrs. Simmons smiled and took Sally's face in her hands. "But your place is with Tommy now. You'll see this as you grow."

Her reassurance made the emotion of the moment easier for Sally. The newlyweds continued down the aisle, greeted the long line of visitors and guests, then went back to the Simmons house for the reception.

It was also a proud moment for Sally's dad, who was a highly regarded local resident. Mr. Simmons was a data processing supervisor who, like Tommy's dad, worked for the Indiana Public Service Company for many years.

When things finally quieted down, the newlyweds packed their car with wedding gifts and drove toward Chicago. They planned to spend their honeymoon at a nearby Lake Geneva, Wisconsin, resort hotel. It was 4:30 in the morning by the time they got to Lake Geneva, lost and needing directions.

"Let's stop and ask that policeman for directions," Tommy suggested.

"Policeman? Where?" yawned Sally.

"Over there. Parked in the gas station."

Tommy pulled his car alongside the squad car and got out. He walked over to the window and saw the officer was asleep. Tommy tapped on the window. There was no response. He rapped harder. This time the policeman, startled, sat up in the seat and grabbed for his revolver. Tommy stood back, but with both hands in view, cautious.

"Excuse me for bothering you, officer," Tommy explained, "but we're lost. Can you tell me how to get to the Abbey?"

"Wha-what?" the cop blinked and finally stumbled out of the squad car, shining a flashlight into Tommy's face.

"Lemme see your license," he mumbled, trying to recapture his wits.

Tommy showed him his driver's license, even his wedding license, and assured him that he wasn't some escaped convict or axe murderer. When he explained his situation about three more times, the officer finally seemed willing to show the sleepy couple the way to the lodge.

A half hour later the two of them collapsed into bed, tired and exhausted, sleeping soundly until 10:30 the next morning when the alarm rang, reminding them that it was almost time for their boat tour around Lake Geneva with a friend, Jack Childars. Lazily, they ate breakfast in bed, dressed in their bathing suits, and were invigorated by the fresh air of the lake trip.

That night they had dinner at a nearby resort where entertainer Joan Rivers was performing. She had learned about the popular White Sox pitcher and his bride in the audience and "treated" the young couple to a barrage of one-liners about marriage and newlyweds.

The next day, after their day and a half honeymoon, Tommy and Sally left Lake Geneva to go back to Chicago. Reporters at the ball park couldn't believe Tommy would be so devoted to baseball as to interrupt his honeymoon for baseball practice. Tommy didn't bother to explain that they had also returned to go apartment hunting. They wanted to locate something before Tommy was scheduled to go on the road with the team.

After baseball practice, they found an attractive apartment in the southwest Chicago suburb of Lisle, and moved in with their assortment of wedding gifts.

Marriage is an adjustment in itself. The baseball wife, however, is forced to deal with peculiarities that are strange and a bit frightening to a young girl. "Stranded" in a strange city, she had no one to talk with. Tommy called her daily, but Sally found herself phoning her mother long distance several times.

"Mom . . .?"

"Yes, dear?"

"Um . . . could you tell me how to keep mashed potatoes warm? . . . The game's in extra innings."

This was typical of the way a call might begin. After a few minutes of reassuring conversation and advice, Sally would be all right.

Their times together helped make her more comfortable, but she still slept uneasily when Tommy left for out-of-town games. Every out-of-the-ordinary bump or car horn would startle her wide-awake in the middle of the night and send her heart racing.

One factor they had not learned about their apartment complex when they moved in was that some of the units were occupied by so-called swinging singles whose post-midnight parties were also a constant and fearful interruption to her peace of mind.

Tommy was still away on his road trip when she heard noises from a neighbor's party in the hall. It was nearly two in the morning and she tossed uncomfortably in the bed.

Suddenly there was pounding on her door. Sally panicked and sat upright in bed. There was a drunken voice accompanying the pounding. "Hey, you _____, why don't you play for the Cubs instead of those lousy, _____ Sox!" The man's voice was slurred, and muffled through the door, but she heard the obscenities and was by now thoroughly terrified.

The pounding continued for a minute or two and she could hear others laughing but trying to hush the belligerent drunk. Sally's hand reached instinctively for the phone. Should she dial the police, operator—who? Just as instinctively she found her hand dialing the familiar area code and number of the Simmons house in Plainfield.

She emptied all her emotions on her folks, long since asleep. When Sally was coherent enough to reassure them that she was unharmed, they tried to calm her into going back to sleep.

"I can't!" she explained. "I'm coming home!"

"But, darling . . ." her mother interrupted.

"I can't stay here another minute without Tommy! I'm leaving right away!" True to her word, Sally dressed quickly and threw some things in an overnight case. She grabbed her trench coat and raced for her car in the parking lot, all the while praying for God's protection. She drove tearfully for the first one hundred miles, and began to calm only when she crossed the state line into Indiana. It was sunrise as she pulled into the safe and familiar driveway of her parents.

Tommy was understanding and sympathetic, when he learned what Sally had done. "But driving alone in the middle of the night is just as scary as what happened in Lisle," he pointed out. From that time, until she felt more comfortable, Sally traveled to Plainfield and stayed with her folks when Tommy went on the road. Or, once in a while, she would have the rare treat of traveling with him.

"Oh, this is exciting!" she exclaimed as their jet touched down in Washington, D.C. "I've never been anywhere on trips," she bubbled. She was making plans for sight-seeing tours to all the landmarks with Tommy. He slowly shook his head.

"It's a club policy that there'll be no sight-seeing by the players on game days—it's supposed to get them tired out," Tommy reminded her. He could see her disappointment. "But," he continued, "we'll go see our friend Congressman John Myers—maybe he can suggest how you can go see some of the sights." They did get to tour the White House with a friend, Gerald Ford, then Minority Leader of the House. Ford took them to lunch in the House of Representatives restaurant.

Congressman Myers welcomed Tommy and Sally into his Washington office. After chatting for a half hour or so, he said to Sally, "Why don't you take my old car and take in the sights before the game. I keep an old 'clunker' in the Congressional parking lot for just such occasions. I have to leave town on the weekend for a vacation anyway. You can take the car and when you've finished with it, return it to the Congressional lot and leave the keys under the floor mat."

Tommy and Sally shook hands with him and left his office. Tommy took the rental car back to the ball park, and Sally took the congressman's car to go sight-seeing. She was careful to make sure of how far she traveled on the Beltway in order to get back to the ball park by game time.

After a few hours, Sally decided to go back. But she discovered that the Beltway freeway circled the city and she'd lost her sense of direction. She thought it would be a good idea to drive off at the next exit ramp and get better directions. Sally drove several miles without coming to an OFF ramp. Then she spotted one. After slowing and driving off, she looked for signs to guide her to some place where she could get directions.

The exit ramp had no other traffic and seemed to be a dead-end road. Sally pulled the car over and stopped. She couldn't back up and return to the freeway. Nor could she go on. The road seemed to end. She was wondering what to do next when she spotted a long expanse of asphalt about one hundred feet from the dead-end road she was on.

Well, at least that *road goes somewhere,* she told herself, *but I wonder how you get to it.*

She looked at the ground between her car and the asphalt. It seemed level enough, so she drove across the grass and onto the smooth road. Sally turned her car towards a cluster of buildings. She had a strange feeling about this road. There was no other traffic on it and after driving a half mile or so she could see why. There were airplanes parked by the buildings she had seen—she was driving on a runway!

A small twinge of panic grabbed her stomach. She pushed down on the gas pedal to get off the runway as quickly as possible. The planes, as Sally now saw, were military jet fighters. Flight crews were busily working all around and as she drove past, several airmen looked up with surprise.

Finally Sally saw a way to leave the airfield and get onto a "regular street." The buildings she had seen from a distance turned out to be hangars, offices, and barracks. It was some kind of military installation, Sally reasoned.

After driving around, Sally finally saw an exit gate. Military policemen in a guard shack were restricting traffic in and out of the base. Sally drove up and rolled down her car window.

"Excuse me, Officer. Can you tell me how to get back on the Beltway?" she inquired.

The MP put down his clipboard and looked at Sally. His face got a puzzled expression on it as he asked, "How did you get here?"

"Uh . . . I'm lost. I'm looking for the Beltway."

"You didn't come in this gate. How did you get on base?" His voice was authoritative and cold.

Sally pointed toward the airfield. "I turned off the Beltway and came that way. I thought . . ."

"Get out of the car, please, Ma'am," the guard ordered.

"B-but . . . ."

"Please get out of the car!"

Another MP looked up and the two poked warily into the car, checking the floor of the back seat.

Sally got out. One MP took her keys and opened the trunk and searched it carefully, while the other escorted Sally into the guard shack.

"Now, Miss, suppose you tell me what you're doing here. Those signs," he said, gesturing, "are in plain English, aren't they?" They were, of course, but Sally didn't come through the main gate so hadn't seen them:

BOLLING AIR FORCE BASE
Restricted Area

"But I didn't see them—I didn't come this way."

The MP shook his head. "This is the only way in or out. Now suppose you tell me the real story and make it easy on yourself."

Sally felt her eyes welling up with tears. She explained how she'd gotten lost, driven onto the runway, and ended up here. It was all a simple mistake.

"Lady, you'd better come up with a better story than that. You'd have to knock down two fences in order to do what you said. I think you'd better come with me."

Two older officers came into the room to where the MPs had escorted Sally. The four interrogated her while others were searching the old car.

"Where'd you get that car with Congressional license plates?" asked one of the officers. (Little did she know that one of the Air Police had called Congressman Myers's office and found out that he was to be out of town for three weeks. Therefore the officer turned in a report that the congressman's car had possibly been stolen.)

"And you said your name was Sally John, from Chicago, but your

driver's license says Sally Simmons of Plainfield, Indiana," interrupted one of the MPs going through her purse. "Just who are you
anyway, lady?"

"What's this camera for?" asked another MP.

"I was out sight-seeing and taking pictures of Washington landmarks," explained Sally.

The MP opened the camera and jerked out the film, exposing it to
the light and ruining the pictures Sally had taken of the Washington
Monument, Lincoln Memorial and other places around Washington.

It was all too much, too nightmarish. Sally began to cry. "I'm
Sally John . . . my maiden name is Simmons. I've *told* you I drove
onto the base off the Beltway." Exasperated, Sally cried, "Hasn't
anyone here ever heard of the White Sox?"

A young officer, who had just come into the room, looked up.
"Sure. Chicago's in town today to play the Senators."

"That's right. And my husband is Tommy John, a pitcher for the
White Sox. We just got married. I'm his wife and that's Congressman John Myers's car. He's our friend.

"My driver's license with the new name hasn't come yet," Sally
continued. "Call someone and check it out since you don't believe
me." The officer had heard of Tommy John and verified her answers. After discussing the event for an hour, they kindly
apologized and escorted her back to the Beltway and gave her
explicit directions as to how to get back to Robert F. Kennedy
stadium. (When Congressman Myers returned from his vacation and
found out that his car was reported stolen, he didn't bother to check
the Congressional parking lot where Tommy had left it. The car had
been sitting in a stall on the lot for six weeks before an officer
reported it was there.)

The game was nearly over by the time Sally reached the ball park.
She made her way through the bleachers to just behind the visitors'
dugout. Tommy had been looking for her all afternoon and saw her
come in. The expression on his face was a combination of relief and
irritation. It wasn't until after the game that she was able to explain
to him what happened.

It seemed to Sally, when they were back in Lisle, that the adjustments to marriage—and especially being a baseball wife—were not going to be easy. Baseball players worked irregular hours and had virtually no time for social activities. When the team was on the road, wives had to do everything, including the tasks most husbands cared for on the weekends. Yet, she determined to work hard on making it all work, concentrating on her role as wife. She was relieved that she and Tommy had no children yet, because she'd have to be both mother and father during the long road trips. And with being in such an unusual life-style, there were plenty of adjustments to make.

Tommy, meanwhile, was facing his own frustrations. The White Sox were doing no better as a team. When he pitched well, there seemed to be no support in the field. The fans became fickle and got on the players with catcalls and dwindling attendance. Manager Don Gutteridge was fired three-quarters of the way through the season, replaced by Chuck Tanner. Tommy said that Don Gutteridge was a good man, and he was sorry to see him go. When a friend is fired, you feel empty, and that was the way Tommy felt.

Tanner called the team together and offered ideas on how the game should be played, and how the team could mesh and come together for greater effectiveness. The players responded. They wanted to win, but it seemed to be too late. The White Sox just couldn't climb up from the cellar.

Tommy finished the season with a 12–17 record and a 3.28 ERA; he pitched 269 innings, the most of his major league career. He looked forward to the '71 season. The White Sox management worked on trades and talked of coming back with a team that could build itself over the next season.

Meanwhile, Tommy and Sally decided to move to Phoenix. They packed their furnishings and shipped them off to Arizona. They followed in their Chrysler, planning to stop off in California while Tommy completed his reserve drills at George Air Force Base at Victorville, California. They stayed at the nearby Apple Valley Inn, owned by Roy Rogers. During the day, while Tommy put in his time on duty, Sally learned to knit and strummed her guitar and went horseback riding. It was a time of relaxation and fun for her.

As they prepared to leave Victorville, Sally began to pack as Tommy went to the base for duty. She wanted to get an early start, so by 8:00 A.M., she had all the suitcases packed and decided to start to pack the little things in the trunk of the Chrysler.

The wind nearly blew the screen door off its hinges as she stepped outside. She rocked from its force and had to catch her breath. Sally wasn't used to these gusty desert winds.

As she got to the car and opened the trunk, she looked at the suitcases and decided that to make the best use of the space, she'd put Tommy's boots up beside the spare tire. But when she bent over and tried to put them inside, her arms could not reach across the trunk. She climbed inside and put the boots carefully out of the way alongside the spare tire. As she turned to get out, a gust of wind slammed the trunk lid shut, knocking her down inside.

Sally pushed at the trunk lid. It wouldn't budge. She was locked inside. She started to pound on the trunk lid and yell.

"Hey! Somebody help me—I'm locked inside!"

She felt panic. Tommy wasn't expecting her until 4:30 that afternoon, and no one else knew she was here. She fought off claustrophobia and feared she'd suffocate. But as her eyes became adjusted to the darkness, she could see two little cracks of light and knew that at least some air was coming in.

"Help! *Somebody*—get me out!"

There was no answer to her calls for help. Her fists were getting sore from pounding on the trunk lid. It was no use. Was it her imagination, or was it getting hard to breathe? She prayed that there really *was* enough oxygen inside to keep her alive. Sally rose on her knees and tried to force the trunk open with her back. As she strained at the effort, she kept calling out.

Finally she rolled over and rested. For what seemed like hours, she kept calling out, but no one heard her.

"Maybe if I sing I can keep making noise and it'll be easier to keep it up than just yelling," she told herself. She chose the song *Puff the Magic Dragon*, singing it over and over, until she could feel her voice getting hoarse.

Suddenly she heard a sound and the trunk lid opened. The bright sunlight flooded in and momentarily blinded her. But she saw a small man standing beside the car.

"Oh, thank God!" she cried.

"What are you doing in there?" the man scolded. "Don't you know it's dangerous to play in trunks of cars?"

As Sally climbed out of the car, the man saw the "little girl" he'd been lecturing was really a young woman, and he muttered a quick apology.

"Oh, don't apologize; I'm just thankful you came along when you did. I don't know how much longer I could have lasted in there," she told him.

"How long have you been locked inside?" he asked.

Sally looked at her watch. "Almost two hours."

After regaining her composure, Sally drove to the air-force base for lunch with Tommy and told him the story. Tommy laughed so hard he couldn't eat his cheeseburger, but both were thankful that nothing serious had resulted from the mishap. He realized that being married brought several interesting moments.

"They ought to have some kind of safety-release latch on the inside for such emergencies," observed Tommy later that day as the two of them drove towards Phoenix.

They rented an apartment in Phoenix not too far from Sally's aunt and uncle, Jean and Howard Seitz. Her Aunt Jean was a registered nurse on the night shift at a local hospital, and Sally sometimes accompanied her to her job to learn about her work in the cardiac unit.

Tommy rested, went golfing and swimming and busied himself making lamps out of baseball bats. Sally pursued an interest in ceramics and worked on her knitting. She also was learning how to play golf, and she joined Tommy several times on the golf course.

As the year progressed, it became more and more obvious that, as Tommy indicated to a Chicago newspaper reporter, "Marriage is about the greatest thing that's ever happened to me." He and Sally were deeply in love and grew closer as time slipped by.

The lonely road trips were made easier for them both by their happy, loving reunions when Tommy returned. Sally's adjustments to being a baseball wife became easier. She learned to build her life around Tommy when he was home and to pursue her own interests while he was away. Household duties waited until Tommy was on the road.

The few disagreements they had weren't really so much arguments, as differences in personalities and temperament. Tommy, a few years older and more conditioned to the harsher realities of life, seemed resilient and more able to cope with disappointments. Their good friends Gary and Jean Peters moved East when Gary was traded by the White Sox to the Boston Red Sox. Tommy accepted the fact that their friends would be moving out of their lives, probably for good. For Sally, however, the separation was very traumatic and tearful.

Sally wore her feelings on her sleeve, while Tommy was quiet, rarely showing his emotions. While she was comfortable with his silent strength, Sally sometimes wished Tommy would yell at her once in a while. She felt that her world was so small and Tommy's so big. At first she was afraid that she'd have trouble keeping up with her celebrity husband. Tommy wasn't aware of her occasional thoughts of inferiority, however, and inwardly his pride swelled at his wife who was so superior in just about every way.

"She's absolutely amazing," he confided to a friend one day. "She's beautiful, has good organizational talents, can work well in any situation. I *like* her as well as love her, you know? She's probably my best friend as well as my wife. There isn't anything she can't do when she puts her mind to it."

As they relaxed during the off-season in Phoenix, Tommy and Sally found fellowship with other Christians in a local United Methodist Church. The pastor, Dr. Chilton McPheeters, and his wife, Julia, became their good friends as well as spiritual advisors.

About this time, Sally and Tommy began to have some serious thoughts about God, about His apparent plan for their lives together. They reflected on His bringing them together, His protection of them in serious difficulties, and wondered about these spiritual yearnings which they could not as yet fully identify.

Tommy, in spite of the lackluster season, was still a popular White Sox player. Often, he'd be asked to speak at various functions. His talks were positive, but lacked the spiritual depth he wished he could share. Sally, too, sensed a missing dimension to Tommy's witness but didn't know exactly what it was. He was a spokesman for his faith, both on and off the field. His teammates respected his clean-cut Christian values, but few were influenced to make changes in their own lives.

Without knowing it, these experiences marked the beginning of a greater search for spiritual insight and understanding. For the moment, though, they were content to leave the matter in God's hands, trusting that He would somehow show them more, in His own time and way.

On the way to Sarasota for the '71 spring training season, Tommy and Sally stopped in Mobile, Alabama, to visit Eddie Stanky. He was the baseball coach at the University of South Alabama.

"I'm really having trouble," Tommy admitted to his friend and former manager.

"Yes," nodded Stanky. "Part of it's your fault and some of it's because of the team. You can't help what the team or management does—only what you do."

"It's a slump," offered Tommy.

"Maybe. You might be off on the mechanics. Get somebody you have confidence in to watch you and see if you're rushing your motion, or are off somewhere."

"Ray Berres," Tommy volunteered. "Ray's in Wisconsin. I'll tell him to watch me pitch on TV and diagnose any trouble. What else?"

"Well," Stanky thought for a moment, then suggested, "play to get traded."

"Traded? But *why?*"

"Some guys tend to get their heads down and loaf when playing on a bad team. I want you to do everything I taught you—pitch, hit, field, run bases, and hustle. Somebody will see that you're not just an average player and make a good deal for you," Stanky explained.

"Sometimes," Eddie continued, "nobody notices just how good you are, until you play to be traded. The White Sox probably don't have much confidence in anybody right now—it's what happens when you have a lousy season. You can inspire their confidence—or some other team's confidence— by getting out there every day and playing great ball . . . hustle, run, hit—*everything* to prove you really know how to play baseball. *Somebody* will notice."

Tommy nodded appreciatively. Eddie turned to Sally as they were leaving, encouraging her, and kidding Tommy he wasn't nearly good enough to deserve a wonderful girl like Sally. They shook hands and the couple drove on to Sarasota, talking most of the way about Eddie's baseball advice.

"If you did play to be traded, where would you go?" asked Sally.

Tommy shrugged. "Probably to a National League team. It's sort of an unwritten rule that you don't trade in the same league. Most trades are between leagues. I don't know . . . maybe I'd go to Pittsburgh, or Atlanta."

"Oh . . ." observed Sally flatly.

Tommy picked up on her lack of enthusiasm and changed the subject. "Well, let's not think about a trade. I'm going to play the best I can for the Sox. Maybe this year will be better." Then he added, "I guess things couldn't get worse."

They found an apartment in Sarasota and settled in as best they could for spring training. After looking for a church to attend while in Sarasota, they settled on First Baptist Church. Reverend Emmett Johnson and his wife, Patty, became as close to Tommy and Sally as their friends, the McPheeters in Phoenix.

"Tommy," Reverend Johnson said one day, "I'd like to have you share in the Sunday-night service next week."

"Sure," Tommy said, "I'd be glad to."

"I would like you to talk about baseball and God. I'd like you to give your testimony—what God means to you," remarked Reverend Johnson.

On Sunday Tommy addressed the church congregation along the lines of the pastor's request. It was the first time Sally had heard Tommy speak in a church about his faith, and she was impressed.

The next day, Sally was thinking about the incident, and wondering what God might plan for their lives. Lost in thought, she began to mix a batch of Tommy's favorite chocolate chip cookies.

"Preheat oven to 325 degrees," she read from the recipe, and walked over to the gas stove and turned it on. Preoccupied, she did not notice there was no pilot light *poof* igniting the gas for the oven.

Twenty minutes later, the batter mixed and cookies spooned onto sheets, she took them to the stove to bake. She tentatively touched the oven door. It was still cold. She put the cookies down on top of the stove and looked for a book of matches to light the stove, forgetting it was already turned on.

As the match flared, the entire room seemed to explode. Blue flame danced and seared. She was thrown backwards and landed on the floor, stunned and burned.

Sally was unaware of being unconscious, but when she came to, her face was tight and drawn. Pain revived her enough to turn off the gas, but not enough to give her further direction. Sally sat down on the couch and stared disbelievingly at her hands which were now swelling and blistering into big red sores. She looked in the mirror. She had, for some reason, put on her glasses instead of her contact lenses that morning. She shuddered. If she had worn contacts, they probably would have melted to her eyeballs! As it was, the explosion had blistered her entire face, except where the glasses had shielded her eyes from the blast. Her eyebrows, lashes, and the tufts of hair showing outside her bandanna were singed away completely.

She didn't know what to do. In a state of painful shock, Sally pulled a sheet off the bed and covered herself with it, shaking fearfully.

Not too long after the incident Tommy came home. He immediately called the White Sox trainer, Charlie Saad, who rushed to help. Charlie applied healing salve to the burns and reassured Tommy that the burns were not as serious as they looked.

"But when you think of what *might* have happened," observed Sally later, "I guess we can thank God that He protected me."

Sally wore dark glasses and put eyebrows on with makeup until her lashes and eyebrows began to grow out and skin healed. By the end of spring training, the marks of the explosion had almost disappeared.

They had a new apartment back in Chicago, living first in Rosemont, near the busy and noisy O'Hare Airport. They moved later in the season to Palos Hills, a southwest suburb of Chicago, near their friends Chuck and Carol Brinkman. Chuck was a White Sox catcher and worked with Tommy in the bull pen. Carol and Sally often shared the time together when their husbands were on road trips by having dinner or going shopping together.

Ray Berres, watched Tommy frequently on TV, and often offered suggestions for improvement. So did Tommy's good friend, Gail Hopkins, a Kansas City first baseman who had good insights to the game and how to correct bad pitching mechanics.

In spite of the work, and in spite of the added hustle Tommy had put into his game at the suggestion of Eddie Stanky, the season ended poorly for Tommy (he was 13–16) as well as the Sox, who finished third in the Western Division.

At the end of the season, Sally drove to Comiskey Park to pick up Tommy. When Tommy finally came out of the stadium, he was lugging all of his equipment and personal effects.

"Well, say good-bye to Comiskey Park and Chicago," Tommy said as he slid into the car.

"Why?" asked Sally.

"I don't know. Just instinct . . . a ballplayer senses when he'll be traded. Besides, Chuck Tanner usually says to us at the end of the season, 'Have a good winter, stay in shape, and we'll see you in Sarasota.' But he didn't say it to me. No . . . I feel a trade."

Sally didn't know how to treat the word—what it meant. *Trade?*

"I gave Roland Hemond a dime on the way out," Tommy grinned.

"A dime?"

"Yeah. I reminded him that the winter meetings are in Phoenix this year. He can call me if I'm traded . . . it'll only be a local call!"

"Do you still think it'll be to Pittsburgh or Atlanta?"

"Probably."

"Which team would you want to go to?"

"I don't know. Neither one, really. But I'll go where I have to in order to play baseball in the big leagues—somewhere where they'll let me pitch."

7

It's a Long Way From Indiana

Tommy and Sally bought some land in Phoenix and had a home built. Most of the winter was spent decorating and landscaping the house and yard.

In December, the couple was relaxing in their new home, chatting with Dave Nightingale, then a sportswriter for the *Chicago Daily News,* whom they had invited for dinner. During dessert and coffee, the discussion centered around the trade talks by the baseball clubs going on in nearby Scottsdale.

"What's the word you hear, Dave?" Tommy asked.

Nightingale shook his head. "We hear the same rumors. I'd only be guessing, too."

"Think I'll be traded?"

"Yes, I do. I say you'll go to either Pittsburgh or Atlanta. They both need you very badly."

Tommy and Sally looked at each other and blinked. Perhaps it was more obvious than either of them suspected.

"Well, you'll know pretty soon," said the reporter, as he put his coffee cup down. "I'll call you tomorrow," he promised as he stood to leave.

After he left, Sally turned to Tommy. "Either Pittsburgh or Atlanta is about the same to me. Which would you prefer?"

"Of those two? I don't know—I'd have to really think about it," Tommy reflected.

Sally took a different approach. "If you were free to choose which major league team you'd like to play for—any one at all—which one would you pick?"

"That's easy," came his quick reply. "The Los Angeles Dodgers.

They are really a professional club—in every way. The Mets are a good organization too. Yes . . . if I could choose, though, I think I'd pick the Dodgers."

The Dodgers? Sally thought to herself. *But California is half-a-world away from Indiana and our families.*

On December 3, Tommy was outside loading river rocks into a wheelbarrow when the call came from Roland Hemond of the Sox.

"Tommy," he began. "I wanted to tell you that the club has decided to trade you . . . ."

"Yes . . . ?"

"We feel we're in pretty good shape with pitchers. We need hitters."

"Uh-huh . . . ."

Sally crowded next to Tommy to hear the conversation, but the voice was too far away. She pantomimed the question, "Trade?"

Tommy nodded to Sally. She was getting excited. "Where— *where?*" she whispered loudly.

"Well, we've completed a deal and we're getting Richie Allen for you," Hemond continued.

"Hey, that's a *great trade,*" Tommy complimented. "Really— that should really help the ball club this year. Allen's a terrific hitter. And you're right about the pitching. Yes . . . that's a great trade."

"Where? *Where?*" Sally insisted.

"Well, Tommy, I wanted you to know before we announced it to the press. And I want to wish you good luck and know that the trade is nothing personal," Hemond continued.

"Thanks. And I wish you guys the best, too," said Tommy as they hung up. (Hoot Evers had told Tommy never to bad-mouth the club you leave. "It always sounds bad," he would say.)

"What is it? Tell me!" Sally was genuinely excited now.

"I've been traded for Richie Allen," grinned Tommy.

"Is that good? Who does he play for?"

Tommy nodded vigorously. "It's really an answer to prayer. Richie Allen played for the Dodgers. I've been traded to Los Angeles!"

Sally was happy and sad at once. She was thrilled that Tommy's dream of last evening was going to be realized. Yet, she also recalled her observation about the distance between Los Angeles and Plainfield, and Terre Haute. Their parents would probably only get to see them but once or twice a year now.

"Son," Tommy's dad said when they phoned him right away, "it's like going from a Model T to a Cadillac! It's a wonderful trade!"

Before long, Tommy's outdoor project had to be put aside. As the day progressed, the telephone rang constantly. Reporters and commentators from Chicago, Los Angeles, and everywhere between were calling for reactions and comments. Tommy was nearly hoarse by the end of the day, but the two were excited and happy about the turn of events.

Tommy completed his reserve duty at Victorville in early January; then he and Sally drove to Los Angeles for his introduction to the team and club management. The Dodgers had arranged a press conference to introduce Tommy to the local media.

"These things usually go pretty quickly," Tommy explained to Sally. "If you'd like, you can wait here or drive around, while I take care of this."

Sally was tremendously impressed with the beauty of the stadium. It was clean, and even in the midst of winter, was surrounded with lush foliage and green grass. After taking a walk and drinking in the warmth of the sun and sounds of birds in the nearby palms, she drove downtown. Following Sunset Boulevard so as not to lose her way back to the stadium, Sally drove through Hollywood and gawked like any other star-struck tourist. She felt that her drive was rewarded when she actually saw a TV star. Entertainer Tiny Tim, in a big Rolls Royce in the lane next to hers, was the one she recognized.

Back at the ball park, Sally waited for Tommy. He had not counted on the organization and efficiency of the Dodgers. The meeting and press conference was lasting *five hours*. Finally someone asked about Tommy's wife, and he remarked that she was outside in the car.

"Well, by all means, let's bring her in," said Fred Claire, then the Dodger public relations director. In a few minutes, Sally was being photographed with Tommy and introduced to the press. It was an exciting new situation to her, as she and Tommy were becoming celebrities themselves, although neither of them was conscious of it at the time.

Just before spring training in February, it was customary for the Dodgers to play an exhibition game with the U.S.C. (University of Southern California) Trojans. Tommy suited up for the first time in his Dodger uniform, wearing number 25, the same number he had with the White Sox. He walked the darkened runway from the clubhouse to the dugout. As his eyes grew accustomed to the bright sunlight on the field, he looked into the stands. The public had been invited to watch this exhibition game, so he expected to see some fans out on this warm, sunny California day. However, he was amazed to look into the stands and see thirty-five thousand people!

"That's a typical crowd for the U.S.C. game," observed veteran Dodger pitcher Claude Osteen. "The crowds during the season pick up considerably, though."

"I can't believe it. You've got more people here watching *an exhibition game* then we had at Sox park on our best Sunday last year!" Tommy remarked.

"You'll see a lot of difference this year," said Osteen. "The Dodgers really know how to run a ball park."

Later that month, Tommy and Sally drove to Vero Beach, Florida, where the Dodgers held spring training. First, they located an apartment in Glendale, near the ball park.

"But it's so warm in California, you'd think they'd have their spring-training camp there," commented Sally.

"They've got a real good camp near the ocean in Florida, which belonged to the club when they were still in Brooklyn," Tommy explained.

It seemed to Tommy that the Dodgers, more than any other ball club, spent most of spring training concentrating on baseball fundamentals. The players are expected to know the game so well that they react automatically in situations requiring split-second decisions on where to throw, run, hit, and so forth. Tommy had an immediate affinity for Dodger pitching coach, Dwight "Red" Adams, who preached physical fitness and mastery of the mechanics of pitching, building on what Tommy had acquired from

Eddie Stanky and Ray Berres.

Spring training is a time for the ballplayer to limber up, get into physical condition, and sharpen the basic skills. By the time the season starts, the players are eager for the competition. The Dodgers generate a team desire for performance. If an individual doesn't play his best, he is promptly replaced. A player is *expected* to play well, just like the Dodger players of years gone by.

In 1972, however, the season began with a players' strike. In order to stay in shape, some Dodgers went to Santa Monica to work out, others went to Orange County. Simulated games were played between members of the team, while waiting for the season to get under way.

The strike seemed to break the stride of the team. Tommy's first National League game was against the Braves in Atlanta. He was somewhat nervous and the first few innings were shaky. Then, with one out in the third, a ground ball was hit to the infield. The second baseman, Jim Lefebvre, stood on the bag, whipped the ball to first and got an easy double play. Tommy, reassured at the backup support of his teammates, relaxed. "These guys can really play solid baseball," said Tommy. He pitched 7 strong innings, leaving the game for a pinch hitter leading 2–1.

"It's a learning process," Tommy said to Sally about his new assignment. "I'm learning a lot about the Dodgers and the National League."

"Is it different?" she asked.

He nodded. "National League batters seem to be better . . . more aggressive—well, maybe not better, but at least more aggressive."

"Is the pitching any different?" asked Sally.

"The umpires call the low strike more consistently. With the low strike called more consistently a pitcher has to concentrate on the low ball. It should help me because I have a good sinker."

Dodger pitcher Don Sutton and his wife, Patti, called one day to invite Tommy and Sally to go to church with them on Sunday.

"The church is in Burbank," Don explained. "We can go and still get to batting practice on time for the Sunday game."

Tommy shrugged. "Sure. We'll go with you."

On Sunday, the four of them visited the Burbank Evangelical Free Church. Rev. Lareau Lindquist was the pastor. Tommy and Sally saw immediately why Don and Patti were so enthusiastic about the church and its minister.

The service was somewhat typical in many respects—music, prayer and the usual format elements. But it was the sermon that captured Tommy and Sally. The minister seemed to have an uncanny sense of what his congregation's needs were. He spoke in a practical, friendly manner and gave helpful, sometimes humorous, applications of Bible passages for his listeners. Tommy and Sally had never heard the Bible explained so vividly or with so much relevance to their own needs.

They continued to go to the Burbank Free Church and found their faith strengthened through Lareau Lindquist's sermons, and their spiritual understanding widened as they began to study the Bible and read other Christian books.

This gave way to a personal devotional life that had been neglected. Their hunger for the things of God became an important part of their lives.

Now their days concluded with a time of shared thoughts and prayers. Before going to sleep at night, Tommy and Sally would lie in bed, read to each other from the Bible, then pray together. However, instead of rituallike addresses from some written liturgy, their prayers had a personal dynamic. Holding hands, the two of them conversed with God.

In May, the Giants came to town for a series. Los Angeles had acquired catcher Dick Dietz from the Giants, and Manager Walt Alston called a team meeting before the game to discuss how to pitch to the Giant batters. After the meeting, pitching coach Red Adams stopped Tommy.

"I almost pulled you out of that meeting," he said.

"Why?"

"Because," Adams explained, "I'm afraid all that talk about how to pitch the Giants will subconsciously affect your game."

"I think you're right, Red. I'd say just let a pitcher do his own pitching—let the batter adjust to him and not the pitcher to the batter.''

From that time, the Dodgers excused the pitchers from such team meetings. They were free to concentrate and plan with the catcher how best to pitch.

Red's advice to Tommy on the mound proved helpful too. Tommy for so long had been with teams that didn't score many runs. His lifetime ERA of under 3.00 had proved that he deserved more wins than he had.

On May 23, after a Giant game, however, Tommy encountered one of the occupational hazards of pitching. His elbow was painful as he pitched. The club doctor diagnosed the problem as bone chips after looking at Xrays of Tommy's arm.

''The chips really shouldn't cause real problems before the end of the season because they're not being pinched in the joint surfaces,'' said Dr. Frank Jobe, the team's specialist. ''We'll give you injections to relieve the inflammation while you pitch for the rest of the year, and we can do surgery, if need be, in the fall.''

''How bad is it?'' questioned Tommy, somewhat concerned.

''It's hard to say without surgery. But I wouldn't worry,'' smiled the doctor. ''We'll get it done in the fall early enough so you'll be able to start next season.''

''The human arm was not designed to throw a baseball,'' Tommy explained to Sally later. ''Bone chips are knocked loose in the joint and then they sort of drift around. That's what causes the pain.''

''And you have to have an operation to get the chips out?''

Tommy nodded. ''It should be pretty routine.''

Sally had gone along with Tommy for the Xrays and had Dr. Jobe look at her feet as well.

''I've had a lot of pain in my heels when I walk,'' she explained.

Doctor Jobe examined her, took Xrays and found calcium-deposit spurs on her heel bones. ''Looks like we'll have 'his and her' beds at the hospital,'' he joked.

''Oh, I don't want to wait until fall,'' Sally said. ''Can't I have my operation right away?''

Sally was admitted to the hospital and came through surgery successfully. Patti Sutton and a couple other friends came by to visit. As they listened to the Dodger game on radio, announcer Vin Scully told listeners, "Pitcher Tommy John is really on target tonight. He has just struck out Atlanta's ace, Hank Aaron, for Tommy's 1,000th career strikeout."

The wives all cheered, forgetting momentarily that they were in a hospital.

A tall, handsome man in pajamas and robe, walking nervously down the hall, was distracted by the cheers and laughter coming from the room. He looked inside and saw the radio.

"Is that the Dodgers game?"

"Sure is," said Sally. "Come on in and listen."

The patient introduced himself as Bob Cohen and flirted good-naturedly with the women, none of whom had yet introduced themselves.

"Are you here for surgery?" asked Sally.

Bob nodded. "Tomorrow morning—on my knee."

"Who's your doctor?"

"Jobe," Bob answered.

"Oh, well, then you don't have to worry. He's the greatest."

Just then Vin Scully, on the radio, interrupted, "Incidentally, while we're talking about Tommy John, we ought to mention that his lovely wife, Sally, is recovering from foot surgery and we send her our best wishes for a speedy return to home and family."

Bob Cohen stared at the radio, looked at Sally, then the other wives. "Are you Sally John?" he asked.

"That's me," she replied, laughing. Bob was thrilled to be meeting a wife of a Dodger ballplayer.

Later that night, when Tommy came to see Sally, she sent him down to say hello to Bob and wish him luck with his surgery.

By the July All-Star Game break, Tommy's record was 8–5. A couple of weeks later, while pitching against the Dodgers' archrival, Cincinnati, the hard-hitting Reds, Tommy emerged with a phenomenal 13 strikeouts.

By the end of the season, Tommy had won his stripes as a Dodger. There may have been other pitchers and fans who initially showed disappointment: "Who's Tommy John and why'd they trade Richie Allen?" However, he was now accepted as an effective pitcher. Tommy's record for the 1972 season was 11–5, with 13 "no decisions." In 7 of these he was leading when taken out of the game. On September 22, in a game he pitched against the Giants, he slid into home plate and jammed his elbow. A bone fragment was knocked into the area of the ulnar nerve ("funny bone") and Dr. Jobe decided to push up the surgery.

The night before his scheduled arm operation, Sally came to visit Tommy at Centinela hospital. Everyone, including Dr. Jobe, reassured them regarding the operation. Sally was not worried because Tommy seemed relaxed and unafraid.

"You're not even a little bit scared?" she smiled.

"It's goofy—but I'm actually looking forward to it," Tommy replied. "The sooner it's done, the sooner I can start playing baseball again."

The minister of the Burbank Free Church, "Lash Lareau," as Tommy nicknamed his new friend, came by to visit on his hospital rounds. He kidded Tommy a bit, prayed briefly, then waved. "I've got to go see some *sick* people."

When Sally left after visiting hours, Tommy lay back in the semidarkened hospital room and stared at the ceiling. *Almost all pitchers have some difficulty with their elbows or arms,* he reminded himself. Without the operation, Tommy knew he'd never pitch well again. It was as close as he'd ever come to seeing his major league baseball career suddenly cut off. The thought of never pitching again momentarily frightened him. Tommy rudely pushed the thought from his mind, trying to concentrate on the positive elements of Lareau's prayer. He reminded himself that everyone had given him assurances that he *would* pitch again—the bone-chip removal surgery should be routine, successful, and he'd be throwing again in a couple of months. Tommy closed his eyes and focused his thoughts on this—that he'd be throwing again by January. *It's in Your hands, Lord,* he prayed, then fell asleep.

The surgery *was* routine and successful. Surgeons removed a large bone fragment from his arm-muscle tissue. When Tommy awoke, his left arm was in a cast. He was "starving," craving a Big Mac from nearby McDonald's, after not eating since six the previous day. Doctor Jobe came into the room and smiled at him.

"The surgery went very well," the doctor grinned. "Nothing out of the ordinary. We'll take off the cast in two weeks and you'll be able to work out slowly." A teammate, Frank Robinson, came to visit Tommy with an armload of magazines and candy, cheering him up.

By Thanksgiving, Tommy was exercising his arm and playing catch with Sally. The cast was gone and the strength was returning. During December he gingerly tried pitching. By January, just as planned, he was throwing pretty well.

In February, as Tommy and Sally drove to Vero Beach for spring training, once again they stopped in Mobile to visit their friend, Eddie Stanky.

"How's the arm, young man?" Eddie asked. In spite of their growing friendship, Eddie alway addressed Tommy as "young man."

"Oh, the arm's fine," Tommy offered.

"Great. But you remember—only pitch when you're ready. Don't rush things. You'll be in a fishbowl as it is. Everyone'll be lookin' at you to see if you really still have your stuff. Don't let it get to you," Eddie advised.

"You know," he added, "being traded to the Dodgers was really the break you needed. This should really be a great year for you. Maybe you remember I played for the Dodgers myself—in the forties. Anyway, you'll have over 160 games to prove yourself. Don't rush your arm. Pitch when *you're* ready."

They chatted for quite a while as Tommy and Sally brought Eddie up to date with all the other exciting things happening in their lives.

"You know," Eddie suggested, "if you're going to be living in Los Angeles, you ought to get a dog for Sally."

"A dog?" Tommy asked.

Sally gasped, adding, "But we already have a Siamese cat—Charlie."

"No, I mean a watchdog," Eddie explained. "Tommy—you're on the road a great deal of the year. Get Sally a watchdog—you'll both sleep better."

Tommy looked at Sally who shrugged.

"You both are from fairly small towns in Indiana where you never even locked your doors at night. But Los Angeles . . . any big city

. . . is different," observed Eddie.

Sally recalled the incident earlier in Chicago where the drunk pounded on their apartment door in the middle of the night, terrifying her.

"Maybe you're right, Eddie," said Tommy. "We'll look into it."

Both Tommy and Sally were tired by the time they got to Vero Beach. They unpacked quickly and collapsed into bed, but Tommy was restless. He knew that he'd have to prove himself all over again when he reported in the morning for spring training. Tommy being disabled at the end of last season had forced the club to call on other pitchers to fill in. Each of them was as serious about holding on to a position as "starting Dodger pitcher" as the other. Competition would be friendly, but determined. No one would willingly give Tommy his place back on the team.

Unconsciously Tommy rubbed his elbow. He knew it was mended and he could put the arm operation behind him. *Tomorrow,* he thought, *I'll show them I can still pitch.*

The Dodgers' management works to see that everyone in the organization is happy and comfortable at spring training. Although wives could not live "on base," they were welcome during the workouts and drills, and usually stayed nearby in condominiums on the ocean. Wives of head-office personnel tried to help the players' wives feel a part of the "family." Sally became friends with Bess Campanis, wife of Al Campanis, the Vice-President of Player Personnel for the Dodgers. (Sally would be devastated and grief-stricken at the loss of her friend Bess to cancer just a few years later.) However, now the two of them chatted, shopped, and exchanged recipes while their men were busy about the details of professional baseball.

Sally was unaware of the tension in the Dodger camp. The coaches and manager were watching their pitchers limber up and get back in the groove of the season. During batting practice and intra-squad games they made notes on clipboards and chatted quietly to each other out of earshot of the players.

"How's Tommy's arm?"

"He *says* it's fine—that he's ready to pitch."

"What do *you* think?"

"I don't know. He *looks* okay. The mechanics . . . ."

"Has he still got big league stuff?"

"Seems to . . . ."

"Well, you never know about the arm. Sometimes you get it back . . . sometimes you don't."

In his first game, against the Minnesota Twins on a windy March day, Tommy gave up 6 runs. Whispers and rumors spread quickly through the camp.

"Do you suppose Tommy is through in the big leagues?"

"Do you think his arm is gone?"

It was impossible for Tommy to be unaware of the questions, the doubts. Everyone was asking—some out of concern—and perhaps some of the younger pitchers were wondering about their own position if Tommy was chosen as a starter. Even the sportswriters were stopping by to inquire "How's the arm?"

Finally, after an exhibition game at Orlando, Tommy reached the breaking point when two reporters came over to ask about his elbow.

"Look, I struck out 13 Cincinnati Reds in one game last year with bone chips in my elbow, and you guys didn't come around and ask me how my elbow felt then. Nobody in the stands, on the bench, or in the press box can tell me how my arm feels, or when I'm ready to pitch again! I'm not going to hurt my arm trying to 'prove' something to management or to impress some coach. I've been around long enough, and I'm smart enough not to do too much, too soon. I'll be ready to throw when the season starts."

The two men blinked and backed up a few steps. Immediately Tommy regretted his angry outburst but made no apologies.

Tommy stalked away and took six new baseballs from the bag in the dugout. He called to one of the young catchers, Kevin Pasley.

"Will you catch me while I warm up?"

The catcher nodded and they walked to the bull-pen area. After a few warm-up pitches, Tommy began to really test his arm. He was throwing his fast ball as hard as he could. He threw curves—and they were breaking across the plate, just as they were supposed to do. He mixed up his pitches, alternating curves and fast balls.

Perspiration rained from his hair and head as Tommy put every ounce of energy into each pitch. He kept this up for an hour.

"Hey, Tommy—let's quit for now," called the catcher. "My hand is sore."

"Okay," Tommy muttered.

"Well, you've still got it, T.J. Your arm's just great," his team-mate said. "But . . . ."

"But what? asked Tommy curtly.

"Well, just don't try too hard," he said walking away after slapping Tommy affectionately on his backside.

Tommy grinned. "Thanks. Thanks for catching me."

Inside the clubhouse Tommy routinely iced down his arm and thought about his day. His arm felt good—it wasn't just bravado. There was no muscular pain that night either, only the usual stiffness and soreness, which would be worked out as the season continued.

The next day Tommy apologized to the two reporters he'd yelled at the day before. Then he repeated the routine of the previous day. He pitched vigorously for over an hour, curves, fast balls, changes—then iced down his arm. Confident that he'd earn back his starting position, he continued this routine until the official season started. Walt Alston still had not decided on his five starting pitchers for the '73 season. That meant Tommy could demonstrate his ability in several league games, while Alston decided who his five starters would be.

The Dodgers lost their first two games. Tommy started the third game of the season and pitched a shutout. The team lost their next four games. Tommy's turn to pitch came again, and once again the Dodgers won. Tommy's record was now 2–0.

Tommy was relaxed now as the managers and coaches discussed the pitching rotation. With his record, he felt secure as one of the five starters of the six pitchers who were vying for the starting rotation. One would be assigned to the bull pen to await an injury or illness of one of the others. Tommy would feel sorry for whoever had to pull the bull-pen assignment. It was boring, frustrating, and difficult to sit by and watch others play. In addition, the lack of regular pitching caused the extra starting pitcher to get rusty.

"Hey, Tommy!"

Tommy heard someone yelling at him and turned. He recognized a Los Angeles reporter.

"Tommy, do you have a minute?"

"Sure."

The sportswriter came over and took out a small cassette tape recorder and began to interview Tommy. "What are your thoughts about being assigned to the bull pen? Do you think Walt Alston has some doubts about your arm operation—is that why he's not naming you as one of his starters?"

The questions caught Tommy by surprise. He motioned for the man to turn off his recorder.

"Where'd you get your information?" Tommy asked sharply.

"Alston—he's given us the names of his starters and you're pegged for bull-pen duty."

"It's the first I've heard . . . ."

The writer jumped back in. "Well, what are your thoughts about . . . ?"

"No comment until I find out what's going on," called Tommy, walking toward the dugout.

"Red!" Tommy called. His pitching coach looked up and smiled.

"Yeah—how're you doing, T.J.?"

"Red, is it true?"

"What?"

"That I've been assigned to the bull pen?"

Red shuffled and blinked uncomfortably. "Well, yes . . . ." Tommy's irritation was becoming obvious. "How come I wasn't told? Why did I have to hear it from the press?"

Red shook his head. "I'm sorry, T.J. I thought Walt told you."

"Nobody told me."

"Well, Walt wants to go with Sutton, Messersmith, Osteen, and Downing for now. It's probably for the best, T.J. It'll give your arm some rest and give you a little more time." Red turned and walked out to where batting practice was beginning.

"Well, Tommy?"

Tommy turned toward the voice and saw that the sportswriter had followed him over. "What's the story?" he asked, expecting a sensational interview for his audience.

"Well, the story is this," replied Tommy. He went on to explain how the Dodgers are gifted with many outstanding players and how difficult the job of management must be in trying to assess the talents of players.

"Some of us will go to the bull pen for a while as a result," Tommy shrugged simply. "That's known as seniority."

"If you ask me," the reporter muttered, "I'd say the Dodgers put Tommy John in the bull pen because they know he's Mr. Nice Guy who won't spout off to the press. Tommy John is loyal to the club and they know he won't go yelling and complaining to reporters!"

Tommy smiled, "No . . . I think they want to go easy on my arm awhile, that's all."

The reporter didn't seem entirely convinced, but thanked Tommy and walked away, looking for more interesting news.

Tommy decided this was just another setback and hoped it would work toward the betterment of Tommy John. He pitched on the sidelines every day. They told him not to overuse his arm but they weren't going to use him in relief, so he had to pitch somewhere. He had to keep up his rhythm and would just have to wait until he could start again. Luckily, he had to wait only ten days, and was back in the starting rotation.

Tommy and Sally had taken Eddie Stanky's advice and bought a black German shepherd. Sally named the dog "Sally's Princess Bonnie Blue," after the little girl she'd read about in *Gone With the Wind*. Bonnie was a lot of fun and Tommy kept his mind off his frustrations by running with her and playing Frisbee with her. She became very important to them.

On Sundays, Tommy and Sally continued to attend Lareau Lindquist's church.

"You know," Tommy told Lareau one day, "I've learned more of the Bible from you in a year than the past twenty-four years of going to church put together."

Lareau simply smiled.

"And the people of the church are great, too. They treat you like a friend, a neighbor, instead of a baseball player first and human being second, like most people do," Tommy reflected.

Lareau knew exactly what Tommy meant. The spotlight of fame that the public puts on baseball players is great—and good for the ego. But the public attention can be fickle. Few people cared for them as Christian friends first and baseball players second.

Many times being a celebrity has its benefits. As an avid golfer, Tommy had for years played in various Pro-Am tournaments. The one he longed to play in was the prestigious Bing Crosby Pebble Beach Pro-Am Tournament. After becoming a Dodger, Tommy received a personal invitation from Bing Crosby to come up and play. Tommy lost no time in thinking it over and has played in every tournament but one since. He also enjoys the Joe Garagiola's Tucson Open, the American Airlines Tournament, the Nashville Music City Open, the Glen Campbell L.A. Open, plus several charity golf tournaments.

Tommy was getting very little recognition from the press, however. He was pitching consistently now, in and out of the bull pen. He had convinced management and his teammates that his arm had definitely healed, although probably no one had as much confidence in it as Tommy. He was always being in the position of proving himself. A rival ballplayer once complimented Tommy on his pitching in a way that bolstered his confidence in his arm even more. Rusty Staub, an outfielder for the New York Mets, told Tommy, "You know, there are a lot of pitchers who can collar* a batter. None of us likes to be caught swinging or looking at a third strike. You're just as mean, but you don't make us look as bad. It's a 'comfortable collar,' even though when I get up to bat I know you're going to throw every kind of pitch in every conceivable spot. Once in a while you even let us hit it to the outfield."

By the end of the season, Tommy had one of the best years ever in his baseball career. He had a 16–7 record and was the league percentage leader for 1973—a statistic compiled for pitchers with 15 or more decisions. Tommy's name went into the record book alongside other Dodger greats—Preacher Roe, Carl Erskine, Don Newcombe, and Sandy Koufax.

"With such a good year you ought to ask for a better contract next time," suggested Sally.

"I *should* be able to get a raise, but contract renewal is the worst

* A "collar" is going without a hit; a "comfortable collar" is going to the plate and making contact with the pitch while making an out.

time of year for me. I can't go in and play those little games back and forth for six weeks. I don't like to hear how poorly I've been doing all of a sudden and then tell them how 'great' I am. I wish there was a better way.''

''Why not call Bob Cohen and see if he'll advise you on negotiations with the Dodgers?'' Sally offered.

''Bob Cohen—our friend from the hospital?''

''Uh-huh. He's a successful attorney and represents other clients like you in contract negotiations. Why don't you call him?''

7Tommy talked with Bob Cohen by phone and explained his ideas and aspirations for continuing in major league baseball. Bob took mental notes and questioned Tommy closely about his efforts for the Dodgers. When they finished, Tommy had tremendous respect for his new attorney. Bob Cohen drew from Tommy a confidence in his own ability that was difficult for Tommy, because of his shyness, to personally verbalize.

''Let's face it, Sally,'' Bob Cohen had said in one of his phone calls to her, ''Tommy is basically a shy person. His modesty and humility are good human qualities—that is, until it's time to talk contract.''

''What do you mean?'' Sally asked him.

''Well, you know that Tommy doesn't talk about his own record, his own statistics. After all, he led the league with his won-loss percentage, didn't he? He only talks about the Dodgers—about team effort—how well the *team* is doing.''

''We'll have to encourage him to change a little bit and pat himself on the back for the Dodgers. He deserves some of the credit, too,'' Sally added.

Tommy went in to meet with the Dodger management and, on the basis of Sally's and Bob Cohen's suggestions, was able to improve his contract with the team.

Tommy and Sally decided to live year-round in the Los Angeles area. They sold their home in Arizona and bought a ranch-style house in Yorba Linda, in Orange County. Their new home is situated on a beautiful golf course and has nearly three-fourths of an acre, room for Bonnie, now a full-grown German shepherd, to run. For prespring-training workouts, whenever a catcher wasn't available, Tommy pinned a tarpaulin to the chain link fence and threw at painted "spots" as pitching targets in the backyard.

One of the things they missed, however, was the Evangelical Free Church in Burbank, and Lareau's sermons. It had been almost a year since they had attended his church and now went to another church in the area. But somehow it lacked the vitality of their former place of worship and Bible study. As a result, it became easier to skip Sunday services occasionally. Soon, church attendance was the exception rather than the rule. Tommy's busy baseball schedule was his justification for skipping church. It was not long before he rationalized that he was also too busy for personal Bible study.

Sally, however, felt their spiritual lives were lacking.

"Back in Chicago, you always shared your faith with others—at churches and even among the White Sox players," she observed.

"Well, that was different," Tommy said. "I can't discuss my Christianity with the Dodgers players. They're different—more sophisticated than the guys in Chicago were."

"But don't you think you have a responsibility to say something for the Lord?" Sally asked.

"Yes . . ." Tommy admitted, "but sometimes I don't get the right opportunity. I feel when the time is right, I can witness to the guys about Christ and they'll listen. God's timing is best. He knows when and where and what I should say—you know?"

"Well, let's pray that God will give you that opportunity," Sally suggested.

8

Joy and Tragedy

Things never looked brighter for Tommy and Sally as New Year's Eve ushered in 1974. It was their first holiday season in their new home, and already they had met many new friends and neighbors.

Their church life, which had gone a bit sour during the past year, improved considerably when one day they received an unexpected note from Lareau Lindquist.

> Dear Tommy and Sally,
>
> Evie and I have just answered a call to the Evangelical Free Church of Yorba Linda. I learned that you and Sally recently moved here too. If you have not as yet found a church home, we'd be delighted if you'd join with us in worship.
>
> Cordially in Christ,
>
> LAREAU

It was a renewing experience to sit in the congregation once more and listen to Lareau preach. Both Tommy and Sally often shared the uncanny sensation that Lareau was indeed preaching the Word of God and that God was speaking through him directly to Sally or Tommy.

"I know Lareau couldn't possibly have known what I was thinking and feeling," Sally said one evening. "I'm sure God knew, though, and used Lareau to speak directly to me."

Tommy nodded. More than once he had experienced the same "coincidence."

Now, here at the beginning of the New Year, Tommy paused to reflect on his good fortune. He was thankful—for not only the material things, such as their new home and attractive salary—but for those intangible spiritual values as well.

He looked forward to a great new baseball season and promised himself to do everything possible to earn his increased salary. His enthusiasm and confidence were shared by the rest of the team. The club had completed a couple of trades and was building a strong player organization. It was only spring training, but already the players were talking of World Series possibilities.

One game in particular during spring training seemed to establish for Tommy the kind of year it was going to be. At Vero Beach, he pitched against the St. Louis Cardinals. Fifteen men came to bat in the first 5 innings and all 15 were put out—on fewer than 40 pitches.

Don Sutton opened the regular season with a shutout against San Diego, 8–0. Tommy was to pitch the second game. He also pitched an 8–0 shutout.

By April Tommy had 5 starts and his record was 5–0, with 2 shutouts. He tied Koufax's record of 5 wins in one month.

"It's incredible!" Tommy excitedly told Sally after his 1–0 shutout of Philadelphia. "It's the kind of year every pitcher dreams he's going to have. I *know* it! I know this has got to be my best year ever!"

Tommy lost just 3 games by the middle of July. His record now stood at 13–3, with a 2.58 ERA. With eleven weeks remaining in the season, he could easily win 20 games, perhaps more, and continue to help the Dodgers in their pennant drive and World Series aspirations.

Sally had added to Tommy's "good" year by announcing the fact that Tommy would become a father in September. They were both excited and began to prepare for the new addition to their family. They decorated the nursery, shopped for a crib, layette, and diapers, thoroughly enjoying their new roles as parents-to-be.

By now, the swelling in her abdomen was just beginning to show. Tommy kidded Sally about her tiny bulge as they rode toward

Dodger Stadium for Tommy's last game before the All-Star break.
They also talked about their disappointment at Tommy's not being
included on the '74 All-Star Team.

"I don't understand it," said Sally. "You have the best record in
the National League. Why didn't Yogi Berra pick you for the team?"

"Well," answered Tommy, "you have to learn not to count on
things like that. Baseball is not always logical."

"But I'm disappointed," Sally said sharply. "In fact, I'm *mad!*
It's just not fair!"

Tommy smiled ruefully. "Yes . . . I'm upset, too," he admitted.
"It's a big disappointment, but I'll just keep plugging along and try
to win 20 or 25 games. Maybe next year . . . ."

Sally went to sit in the stands with the other players' wives while
Tommy dressed for the game. As the game began, Dodger an-
nouncer Vin Scully also expressed disappointment at the fact
Tommy was overlooked in the All-Star appointments.

"I think Dodger fans ought to write the Baseball Commissioner on
this. Here's a young man with the best record in the National
League and he's ignored. You can do something by writing the
Commissioner and asking to have Tommy John appointed to the
team," he announced.

Tommy humbly acknowledged the fans' cheers as he walked to
the mound to face the first few Montreal batters.

The game began routinely for the first few innings. The Dodgers
led 4–0 at the end of three innings. The first Montreal batter in the
fourth inning was Willie Davis. He tapped an infield grounder and
beat the throw to first base for a base hit. On a 3–2 count, Tommy
walked Bob Bailey, the next batter, and concentrated on the third
man, Hal Breeden. Tommy stole a glance at the two runners on base
and went into his motion, intent on throwing a sinker to Breeden.

As his arm arched and spun forward, a tearing sensation surged
through Tommy's elbow. He had the horrible feeling that his arm
had somehow been ripped from its socket and was flying off at right
angles to his body, and that the ball went off in another direction.

Tommy stumbled slightly, but regained his balance and completed
the pitching motion. The ball hadn't really soared into space. It was

a little wild, but the catcher caught it. Tommy looked at his arm, still attached soundly to his shoulder.

It was a surrealistic sensation, almost like a dream. Did he experience something in his arm or didn't he? He felt no real pain. He could move his arm all right.

Checking the base runners again, Tommy got on the mound once more. *I'll try the sinker again,* he thought. He completed his motion and unleashed the ball a second time. This time the sensation was more intense, more real. Tommy thought he even heard a "slamming" sound as his arm snapped forward. Again he had the unnerving feeling that he had thrown his arm off his body and the ball into the stands.

"Time!" Tommy called to the home plate umpire, knowing something was wrong.

"What's the matter, T.J.?" Manager Walt Alston asked, hurrying toward Tommy on the mound.

"You'd better get somebody up in the bull pen—I hurt my arm, Walt," he said simply, grabbing his warm-up jacket from the dugout and continuing toward the clubhouse.

Bill Buhler, the Dodger trainer, rushed up. "Let's go find Dr. Jobe," Tommy said to him, still hurrying toward the clubhouse. At first base, Steve Garvey had a strange feeling in the pit of his stomach as he watched his friend walk off the mound. Instinct told him Tommy had done something serious to his arm.

In the stands Sally saw Tommy leave the mound. She felt her stomach knot up. *Did he hurt his arm?*

When Tommy grabbed his jacket, she knew something was wrong. "Excuse me," she said, getting up and rushing down to the Dodger clubhouse.

By the time Tommy reached the top of the runway to the clubhouse, Dr. Jobe was already in the trainers' room.

"Come on in, Tommy," Dr. Jobe said quickly, holding open the door to the trainers' room.

In a few minutes, the room was filled with people—players, trainers, reporters who hurried down to see what happened. By now Tommy's arm was shaking with muscle spasms. Dr. Jobe knew that

Dr. Herbert Stark, a surgeon who specialized in upper extremity surgery, was at the game, so he sent for Dr. Stark and asked him to examine Tommy also.

"Please, everyone wait outside and give us a little room," Dr. Jobe ordered.

After examining the arm, the two doctors told Tommy that they thought he had torn ligaments and muscles about the elbow, but they could not be sure of the amount of damage until other tests, including Xrays, were performed. "Tommy," said Dr. Jobe, "why don't you ice down your arm, go home and rest, then stop by the office tomorrow for a more complete examination with Xrays?"

Sally ignored the "No females" policy of the clubhouse and barged right in to see about Tommy. But she was met outside by Dodger pitchers Al Downing and Don Sutton.

"It's okay, Sally," said Sutton reassuringly. "It's nothing but a pulled muscle or something—he'll be okay. You can wait for him in the stands."

"Are you sure?"

"Yeah. Right now it's bedlam in there with the reporters and all. But he'll be out after he ices down his arm."

"A-all right," Sally said, reluctantly returning to the stands.

Tommy was featured on TV that night as Los Angeles sportscasters told their listeners that muscle spasms and "a probable pulled muscle" took Tommy from the game.

Tommy and Sally both had trouble getting to sleep that night. Sally's sister, Judy, and her husband, Dick Ashton, were visiting from Covington, Indiana. Dick sensed there was something more than a routine pulled muscle wrong with Tommy's arm. He did his best to relieve the tension and keep Tommy's mind off the injury. They talked and joked until 2:00 A.M. But in the dark, quiet hours when everyone had gone to bed, Tommy and Sally lay in bed quietly wondering. Tommy, usually low-key and optimistic no-matter-what, was now moody and deep in thought.

He didn't voice his fears to Sally, but could almost relive the sensation of those two pitches again. Tommy suspected that something serious had happened that day. For the first time in his life, including even his bone-chip operation, Tommy was worried about his pitching arm.

After a fitful night, Tommy rose early and dressed. His forearm was exceptionally tender and his arm was stiff and hard to move.

"I think maybe I've torn some muscles," Tommy said over breakfast, adding, "torn them pretty badly."

Sally didn't answer. She put the coffee pot down on the table, looking outside, across the golf course, but seeing nothing. Tommy interrupted her quiet thoughts.

"I guess I'd better get going," he said. "If I leave now I can miss the rush-hour traffic and catch Dr. Jobe as he comes in the office."

"Do you want me to drive you?"

"No, Honey, Dick is going with me." He flexed his hand and watched the fingers move stiffly, painfully.

"We should be back at the usual time, after the game," Tommy said, kissing Sally fondly before going out the front door toward the garage.

The drive to Dr. Jobe's office took nearly an hour. Tommy fiddled with the car radio, searching for his favorite Country-Western station, but not really hearing. Dick tried to take his mind off his arm problem by small talk and jokes. By the time Tommy saw Dr. Jobe, his arm was quite stiff.

Dr. Jobe took Xrays and conducted other tests. The plain Xrays showed no bone chips but were otherwise inconclusive. It was the stress Xray that pointed out the problem.

"Tommy, it looks pretty bad," the doctor said, shaking his head sadly. "It's a torn ligament, I'm afraid."

"What's that mean for me?"

"Well, complete rest can repair a torn muscle . . . and maybe a ligament if it's torn where it joins to the bone. It may attach back to the bone and heal," Dr. Jobe explained, drawing a quick sketch on a pad. "But if it's a ligament, torn here—in the middle—well . . . ."

"Operation?" Tommy asked.

"Probably, but let's see if Doctor Stark agrees." Both surgeons advised Tommy that the best course of action would be to operate without delay rather than wait to see if it would heal.

"But," asked Tommy, "is there a chance that it will heal with rest, so I can pitch this year?"

"Yes, there is always a chance that it will heal with rest, but not a very good chance."

"Then let's rest it and wait, and maybe it will heal," decided Tommy. "The team needs me this year, and since there is a tiny chance that I might still pitch this year, I want to postpone the operation until I'm convinced it is absolutely necessary."

Tommy rested his arm for three weeks before trying it again. When he tried it out, neighbor Ed Varvello got out his old softball mitt from his garage and joined Tommy for catch every evening for twenty minutes or so. After a week of playing catch with Ed, Tommy visited Dr. Jobe to see when he could rejoin the Dodgers on the road, perhaps to pitch batting practice.

He joined the Dodgers in New York and pitched batting practice for three straight days. He followed this with the therapy that Dodger trainer Bill Buhler uses : 3 minutes of water 114° followed by 30 seconds of ice. He used ultra sound following this.

By the first of September, Tommy felt ready to try to see if he could effectively pitch again. He went to Atlanta with the team, still hoping to regain some ground he lost. He knew 20 wins was out of reach. He longed to pitch in the play-offs and World Series.

At workouts he threw the ball fairly hard. Yet, he knew some of the extra "zip" he had to put on his fast ball just wasn't there—not enough to pitch to Joe Morgan, George Foster, or Greg Luzinski, at least.

Tommy tried to pitch with his arm so heavily wrapped in Ace bandages he could scarcely move it. He was able to throw the ball on level ground, but the mechanics of pitching from a mound made it impossible for him to put the ball where he wanted it to go. The raised mound made it impossible to throw without pain, using the basic mechanics of pitching. Pete Rose of Cincinnati told a national TV audience that with Tommy John, their ace left-handed pitcher out of commission, the Dodgers wouldn't have a chance to win the pennant.

Tommy stayed with the team for the rest of their road trip to San

Francisco, but had all but decided on surgery by the time he came home.

Doctor Jobe and Dr. Stark reexamined Tommy when he got back to Los Angeles, and they agreed that he had torn the ligaments on the inner side of his elbow, and that the only chance he had to ever pitch effectively was to have the ligaments repaired or reconstructed by an operation.

"Look, Tommy," Dr. Jobe said quietly, "we're going to level with you. If it's a torn muscle or slight ligament damage that we can repair, we can do it—in and out quickly.

"But if the ligaments are completely torn, then we will have to replace them with a tendon graft, and that will be a much longer operation."

"Can you fix it?" Tommy asked.

"We think so, Tommy. Doctor Stark and I have discussed this, and we have a plan that should work, but . . . ."

"But what?" asked Tommy impatiently.

"Well, as far as I know, it's never been done on a baseball pitcher's elbow before."

Tommy could feel a knot beginning to grow inside his stomach.

Doctor Jobe continued. "We should be able to make your elbow better, but there is absolutely no guarantee that you'll ever pitch again, Tommy. However, I think there is at least a chance that you can, if everything works out as planned, and if you work very hard."

Never pitch again! was really all that Tommy heard. But he tried to push those words from his thought processes.

"It's serious, Tommy. You go home and talk it over with Sally. I know that you're both praying people. Well, I'd surely pray about this," he said quietly.

"Doctor Jobe," Tommy asked, "just how serious is it? On a scale of one to ten—with ten being the most serious—how would you rate it?"

Without hesitation Dr. Jobe replied, "This is a ten. If I were you, Tommy, I'd think about a new line of work. Do you think you play golf well enough to go on the pro tour?"

Stunned, Tommy went home to discuss the surgery with Sally.

"My arm is very unstable," Tommy told her. "The doctors think the ligament is completely torn, and that the only thing holding it in place is the ulnar nerve and skin. I can probably go for years without too much trouble doing ordinary things like driving, eating, or writing. But I'll never pitch with the damage. There's a remote—very remote—chance they can repair the damage by surgery. But they don't hold out much hope I'll ever pitch again."

Sally cried when she understood the implications. Then, the two of them prayed. At first she felt her prayers only went as far as the ceiling. She was angry with God. "Why?" she asked Him. "Why did You have to let this happen?"

In time she accepted what happened, and despite a lack of answers and reasons, gave herself over to God's will.

"Lord," began Tommy, addressing God as if He were an Indiana neighbor, "we don't understand why this has happened. But we know that You have allowed it for a reason. We know everything that happens to us is for our good. Help us to understand all this and give us peace of mind about it. And, Lord," he concluded, "we pray that You'll give us guidance concerning the operation."

By the following week, both Tommy and Sally were certain that surgery was the next step.

"Baseball is my life," Tommy reflected. "God gave me the gift of throwing a baseball better than most other people. My gift to God is to play baseball the best I can—so I've got to pitch again. And He permitted this injury for some reason. But I really believe that He'll give me back my arm. We've got to try the operation, Sally."

Once decided, Tommy wanted the operation performed at once. If it was successful, he reasoned, the sooner it was done, the quicker he could return to the club—perhaps even by spring training.

Doctor Jobe, however, had different ideas.

"Tommy, this operation will require a lot of skill. And I want to minimize the risks. I want Herb Stark to be present, and we will need trained assistants. I've checked to see when I can get them all together and the first day everyone is free is September twenty-fifth. Doctor Stark will be out of town until then."

It seemed like the end of September would never come. For Sally, the waiting was doubly difficult because of her advancing pregnancy. In fact, the baby's due date was September 28.

Finally, on September 24, Tommy checked into Centinela Hospital in Inglewood. Sally, accompanied by her mother, Opal Simmons, checked into a nearby Hyatt House rather than driving nearly an hour each way back and forth to Centinela Hospital from Yorba Linda.

After dinner, Tommy had been given most of the routine tests and had his arm shaved as part of the pre-op procedures.

"How are *you* doing?" Tommy asked Sally, seeing her discomfort.

"I'm fine—just tired. I'll be all right after a good night's sleep," she sighed.

"Well, if the baby's early," he grinned, "you couldn't be in a handier spot."

"Except that Saint Jude's Hospital is where I'm supposed to go and that's quite a drive from here."

"Doris Haisler of Centinela Hospital has arranged for your doctor to have staff privileges here, if it becomes necessary," Tommy said encouragingly.

After more small talk, their conversation took on a more serious tone. More and more, it seemed lately, they found it easier to bring their concerns to God.

"Lord, we realize our backs are against the wall," Sally prayed. "We're kind of scared, but we want to have faith."

"We pray for Doctor Jobe and the surgeons, Lord," Tommy added. "We ask that You direct their hands and enhance all the skills and talents that You gave them. We also pray that You will be glorified in what happens, Lord. We also pray that You will give us peace. And I pray for Sally, God, that You will give her the rest and strength she needs."

Sally found it was not easy to stay depressed around Tommy. His unflinching confidence could not be matched, but neither could it be dampened by her fear or doubt. She wanted to leave Tommy with some positive word that night and searched her tired mind for something.

Tommy had already convinced himself everything would work out, however, and he encouraged *her*. "Don't worry," he said, "get some sleep and something to eat. Take care of yourself."

"I love you," Sally whispered, kissing him good-bye as the public-address system announced an end to visiting hours.

"Good-night," Tommy answered. "See you tomorrow."

Tommy was awakened early the next morning in order to get him to surgery by 7:00 A.M. Sally and her mother were already there before he was taken to the operating room. Tommy could feel the effects of the anesthetic taking over. He was feeling relaxed, drowsy. Through heavy eyelids he could see the concern and depth of feeling in Sally's eyes, yet his tongue seemed immobilized. His speech was beginning to slur and he knew it wouldn't be long now.

"We'll be praying all the while, Tommy," whispered Sally, kissing his cheek as the attendants came to wheel him away.

Sally bit her lip as Tommy was taken from the room. She recalled Dr. Jobe's quiet explanation of what they might expect.

"If it's a partial tear," he told her, "we can repair it and it should heal all right. If it's torn completely or separated from the bone, there's a chance we can repair that too, but we are not sure he will heal strong enough so he can pitch major league baseball."

Sally remembered how serious his expression got when he told her of the possibility. Sally remembered the words, "We should be able to help, but he may never have a strong enough arm to pitch."

Her thoughts were interrupted by her mother's voice.

"Come on, Honey. Let's go sit in the lounge. You need to get off your feet. Everything will be all right."

As Sally and her mother walked slowly down the hall toward the waiting room, Dr. Frank Jobe was just finishing in the scrub room and leaving for the operating theater. Doctor Stark was also scrubbed and in his "greens," as were the other surgeons who would assist with the operation.

It was almost 7:20 A.M. when the surgeon laid back the skin and subcutaneous tissue.

"The only thing holding his elbow joint together is skin and the nerve running down the channel," an assistant observed.

"Well, let's get a look at the damage," suggested Dr. Jobe.

"It's a very bad injury," said Dr. Stark a few minutes later.

Without wasting any time, Dr. Jobe had exposed the problem; not only was the ligament completely torn and unrecognizable as a structure, but the muscles that arose from the inner side of the arm above the elbow were completely pulled loose, and they had all slipped 2 inches toward the wrist. The ulnar nerve was elongated and bruised. One of the assistants removed the 6 inch long *palmaris longus* tendon from his right wrist and forearm so it could be fashioned into a new ligament for the elbow.

"Only seventy-five percent of the people have this tendon," Dr. Jobe commented. "He is one of the lucky ones."

The operating theater's bright tiled walls reverberated with the sounds of a high-speed drill piercing the bone in Tommy's elbow. Four tiny holes were made in the bones, two above the elbow and two below the elbow joint.

Skillfully, patiently, the doctors worked. They carefully threaded the inelastic tendon through the holes and wove the ends together and sutured them to the bones. Next, they repaired and repositioned the injured muscles. Finally, after almost three hours of tense, painstaking repair, the operation was over.

Sally stood as she saw Dr. Jobe walking down the hall to the waiting room and went to meet him.

"It's okay," he reassured her. "He's in the recovery room and will be waking up in an hour or so."

"What did you find?"

"We found the worst, as we feared. But we transplanted a tendon from his right arm to his pitching . . . uh . . . left arm," he explained. Doctor Jobe looked at Sally. She seemed so vulnerable just now that he wondered how much he should really tell her.

"Sally, it was really bad. I'll tell you—but we need to wait before we tell Tommy. There is a real possibility that he will never pitch again. I'm sorry."

"Are you all right?" he asked her.

"I . . . I'll be all right," she whispered hoarsely.

"I wish I could have given you a better report . . . ." Dr. Jobe tried to encourage, thought better of it, then excused himself.

Sally said, "Is there any chance at all he can pitch?"

"Maybe 1 in 100."

"That's all Tommy will need—a single chance," Sally replied.

Sally went over to her mother and hugged her. "Oh, Mom, poor Tommy. I love him so." Then she walked over to a nearby telephone booth and sat down on the stool inside. After closing the door, she put her head in her hands and began to cry. All the pain, emotion, and anger pent up over the past few months spilled out with salty tears.

"Oh, God . . . *why?* Why are You doing this? *Why?"*

She sobbed uncontrollably for some time. Finally, spent, she sat back staring at the telephone. Mechanically she dropped in a coin and placed a call to Tommy's folks back in Indiana. All three of them cried during the phone conversation.

"Doctor Jobe told me that Tommy would never pitch again. How can I help him find something else to do besides baseball? H-how *can* I? How can *I* do that?" she cried.

Mrs. John tried to comfort her daughter-in-law. "There are times," she explained, "when it doesn't seem to do any good to pray. But that's all we've got, Honey. There's nothing any of us can do except pray. Put it in God's hand."

Tommy began to wake up. His head was spinning and his arms were sore. He found that his thoughts were vivid and mind alert, but he had trouble coordinating his body to respond.

Finally he began to be more aware of his surroundings and smiled when he saw Sally come into his room. She had gone into the ladies' room to freshen her makeup and erase the signs of her tearful outburst earlier. She smiled brightly and genuinely tried to be cheerful.

"Hi . . . would you like some Seven-Up?"

"Yes . . . my throat is really dry." Tommy sucked through the bent straw and felt the cold liquid ease his throat.

"I see they found the worst," Tommy observed. "I knew it when I woke up and found bandages on both arms."

"Yes . . ." whispered Sally.

"Well, I guess we knew it all the time, didn't we?"

"I suppose so."

"How are you feeling? Ready to have a baby yet?" Tommy asked.

Sally laughed. "I'm ready *any* time."

It was almost evening before Dr. Jobe visited again.

"You look like you've put in a long day," smiled Tommy. "Did I louse up your golf game?"

"How are you feeling?"

"Great. I can't believe how good I do feel. When can I go home?"

"Well, let's let the dust settle first. Give us a couple of days anyway."

"What did you actually find in my arm, Doctor Jobe?"

"One of the doctors said he'd never seen anything like it. It was like a bunch of spaghetti in there."

"How long will it take to heal? Will I be able to report for spring training?"

Doctor Jobe hesitated. He had hoped Sally might have prepared Tommy but knew she couldn't have had the time yet. *Oh, God, how do I make this guy understand that he will be extremely fortunate if he ever pitches again?*

"Doctor Jobe?" Tommy repeated.

"Tommy . . . ." Dr. Jobe said quietly. "You have a contract . . . and . . . uh . . . the Dodgers will treat you right. They can carry you the whole '75 season." By being subtle Dr. Jobe hoped Tommy might pick up on what he was saying. But Tommy wasn't on that wavelength.

Sally came back for the evening visiting hours. Tommy was sitting up in bed, clumsily trying to eat supper. His left arm and right one were both wrapped in bandages. He tried to use his right hand to feed himself and the movements were decidedly lacking in gracefulness. But as he progressed, his spills became less frequent.

After supper he pushed aside the tray and tried to get out of bed.

"What are you doing?" Sally called out.

"Have to go to the bathroom," Tommy explained. He stood shakily, then shuffled toward the lavatory.

"Wait, I'll ring for the nurse to help you," Sally said.

"No . . . I can make it myself. The operation is over—now it's up to me. I've got to do it from here on out," Tommy insisted.

On Thursday, the day following surgery, Sally and her mother came to visit. Later in the day, Sally was having strange, uncomfortable sensations shooting through the muscles in her back and pelvic areas.

"You'd better take Sally home," Tommy instructed Mrs. Simmons. "She needs to rest and get ready to go to the hospital herself. The baby is due in two days—she should be home and close to her obstetrician and Saint Jude's Hospital."

It was a long drive to Yorba Linda and Sally insisted on driving, reminding her mother that she could do better on the freeways than Mrs. Simmons, who was used to rural Indiana highways.

At home, Sally learned that those uncomfortable twinges meant the start of labor. She called the doctor who advised her how long to wait before leaving for Saint Jude's.

She tried to phone Tommy at Centinela Hospital but was told no calls could be put through until seven in the morning.

At three minutes before seven Sally called Tommy's room. Groggily he answered.

"Today is the day . . ." Sally began.

"Really? Let me get hold of Doctor Jobe. I want to be there with you!"

"Call me right back, okay?"

Tommy tried to locate Dr. Jobe and finally tracked him down in the hospital operating room.

In a few moments Dr. Jobe answered and Tommy explained his problem.

"Okay," Dr. Jobe conceded, "you can go if someone picks you up and brings you back. I have to change the cast on your left arm and the bandages on your right arm."

Ed Varvello, Tommy's neighbor, drove to Inglewood to pick up Tommy. Then, Ed drove Tommy, Sally and her mother to Saint Jude's, pulling up at the admitting entrance.

A nurse came outside with a wheelchair and started toward Sally. Then she glanced at Tommy, unshaven, with both arms bandaged.

She was momentarily confused and didn't know who needed the wheelchair most!

Laughing, Tommy pointed toward Sally. "She's the one who needs it."

Inside, Sally was admitted and Tommy joined her in the labor room. The doctor arrived shortly and helped Tommy into a surgical gown in order for him to watch the birth of their baby in the delivery room later.

Awestruck, Tommy stood beside Sally when the time came, caught up in the mystical wonder of this unique experience. Their eyes welled with tears at the richness of this moment. Soon a tiny cry broke their reverie.

"It's a girl," announced the doctor.

"A girl," echoed Sally.

"She's beautiful," whispered Tommy.

The next moments were quiet and reverent as Tommy and Sally inwardly thanked God and rejoiced at the beauty and wonder of this exciting event.

Sally and the baby were taken back to their rooms while Ed drove Tommy back to Centinela. He told Dr. Jobe excitedly about his new daughter while the surgeon changed his bandages and put a new cast on his left arm.

Tamara Marie is the name Tommy and Sally settled on later that evening, *Marie* after Opal Marie, Sally's mom. She weighed six pounds and seven ounces.

Sally was relieved and happy when Tami was born. She hoped Tommy would not be disappointed because their first baby was not a boy. But she could see by his expression that it really made no difference—boy or girl—he was a joyous, proud father.

Only later did Sally feel the bitterness and anger she had suppressed. *Why did You let the injury happen to Tommy?* she questioned of God. *Couldn't You punish me instead?*

Tommy did not know her thoughts, but she felt he was reading her mind.

"Look, we can't get discouraged over what's happened. God must have some kind of plan for me, for us, in all this. Let's trust Him to show it to us."

Next to baseball, Tommy likes golf best and plays in numerous tournaments across the country.

At a Pro-Am tournament wi[th]
Pat Boone. *Below:* Tomm[y]
and Sally with Preside[nt]
Gerald Ford.

Two-year-old Tami admires a pretty little girl in the mirror. *Below:* Tami gives her Grandfather Simmons a kiss while Mrs. Simmons looks on with approval.

Mr. and Mrs. Tommy John, Sr. *Below:* Tommy with the greatest of the great: Joe Di-Maggio.

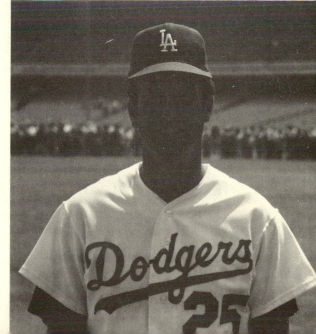

Tommy John III, at two months, looks at the world from under an outsized baseball cap. *Right:* In September 1975, one year after surgery and ready for a comeback. Tommy was on his way to the Arizona Instrucional League.

Showing the form that made him a 20-game winner. (Dodger photo by Mark Malone)

The Dodger starting pitchers: T.J., Don Sutton, Rick Rhoden, Burt Hooton, Doug Rau. *Below:* Jo and Tom Lasorda, Dodger manager.

With that bat she can't miss. Tami with her daddy at Dodger Family Night, 1977.

Shown at the Dinner Show for Multiple Sclerosis, these Athletes for MS: T.J., Al Downing, Reg Smith, Steve Yeager, Burt Hooton, Steve Garvey. *Right:* Tommy in February 1978 with Bonnie Blue, the German shepherd watchdog, who keeps an eye on things while Tommy is on the Road.

9

The Lord Gives—The Lord Takes Away

Within a week after the operation and Tami's birth, while T.J. was home recuperating, the Dodgers had wrapped up their National League division title. Tommy's 13–3 season record, in spite of his injury, was good enough to make him league leader in percentage of games won—for the second year in a row.

Tommy called the clubhouse following the Dodgers' division-clinching win in Houston. Pitching coach Red Adams answered the phone.

"I just wanted to call and congratulate everyone," Tommy explained. "Now you guys can win the pennant, then the Series."

"Hey, thanks, T.J.," Red replied. "We were just talking about you—a lot of the guys were saying we wouldn't be where we are today if it weren't for that lead—you helped us get out front. If we win the play-offs and Series, you'll deserve a great deal of the credit."

Sally insisted the next day that Tommy go to Pittsburgh for the play-offs.

"Red was right. The Dodgers won because of your 13 wins—you should be there. Call Al Campanis [Dodger Vice-President] and ask if you can be with the team," Sally declared.

"Of course, you can," was Campanis's quick answer when Tommy phoned. "In fact," he told Tommy, "I'll go you one better. You travel with the front-office people. The Dodgers will pick up the tab for a first-class airline ticket from Los Angeles to Pittsburgh!"

Baseball policy dictated that because he was not on the active roster, he could sit on the Dodger bench, in uniform, only with the permission of the opposing team.

Danny Murtaugh, Pirates' manager, looked up at Tommy to answer the request.

"Tommy, you have every right to be there. But I'll give permission for you to be there on one condition."

"What's that, Danny?" Tommy inquired.

"That you let me be the first to autograph your cast," Danny grinned. Tommy obliged him and gave him a pen.

The Dodgers played the first two games of the play-offs in Pittsburgh and then were to play the remaining games in Dodger Stadium. Upon leaving Pittsburgh for the West Coast, however, the Dodgers' corporate jet Kay-o II was delayed at the airport for a couple of hours while authorities checked it over.

Someone had phoned to say a bomb was planted aboard to kill the entire Dodger team in flight. After a careful search, no explosives were found, and the team, tired and victorious, left for Los Angeles.

In Los Angeles, Dodger president Peter O'Malley asked Tommy, "Would you throw out the first ball of the West Coast play-offs? We'd like you to do it in honor of what you have done for the team this year."

Tommy was honored by this request from Peter O'Malley. The play-offs of 1974 began at Pittsburgh. The Dodgers won the first 2 games at Pittsburgh and headed back to Los Angeles, needing only 1 more win in the best 3 out of 5 series. Dodger Stadium was decorated beautifully. Banners were displayed and the weather was warm and sunny.

After the bands marched and the fifty-five thousand people were in their seats, John Ramsey announced, "The first ball will be thrown by a man who is a primary reason the Dodgers are here today—*Tommy John.*" Tommy, so handsome in his blue and white Dodger uniform, strode toward the pitching mound—a place he had last seen on July 17—the ball in his right hand, the grim-looking cast on his left arm. You could have heard a pin drop, it was so silent. It was as if people were paying a final farewell tribute to an outstanding pitcher who would probably never pitch again. Sally, her parents, and Tommy's parents were proudly sitting behind home plate. They were so proud but so sorry this was all happening. In their minds, also, they had the terrible feeling they were seeing Tommy on the mound and in uniform for the last time. Tommy drew a deep breath, raised his right arm and threw a perfect strike to begin the West Coast play-offs. As he walked off the mound, he received a standing ovation and doffed his cap to the greatest fans in the world—hoping and praying he was not saying farewell.

The Dodgers went on to beat the Pirates and were on their way to the 1974 World Series.

Oakland grabbed the American League championship that year so the World Series was played exclusively in California.

Tommy felt the sting of being unable to play in the play-offs and World Series. Yet, he felt he was making a general contribution by being there to encourage the team and take movies of the games for later analysis by the coaches and players.

The Oakland As ended up beating the Dodgers in 5 games. This was hard for Tommy to take. He wanted to help the team and he had had many years of experience in pitching against the As. But he had to concentrate on rebuilding his arm—that was the only way to help the Dodgers win—a healthy Tommy John.

Because of his contribution to the team through the first half of the season, Tommy was given a full share of the team's World Series money and his own personalized World Series commemorative ring.

When the excitement of the baseball season was over, Tommy became introspective and thoughtful. Cradling baby Tami in his arms, he would sit and gaze into her tiny face. It gave him strength to persist, because things were increasingly difficult with his recovery.

Tommy visited Dr. Jobe's office weekly for examinations. During one such visit the doctor looked at Tommy's hand and frowned.

"What's this?" he asked Tommy.

"A burn . . . I . . . I guess I'm losing the feeling in my hand. It's like it's asleep. And it's always cold. So the other day I ran it under the hot water to stimulate the circulation in my fingers. But I couldn't feel that the water was scalding hot," explained Tommy.

Doctor Jobe carefully examined his hand and fingers.

"There seems to be something wrong—something we hadn't counted on when we operated. I'm going to send you to a neurologist in Pasadena for some special tests."

After examining Tommy's charts and hand, the neurologist gave him an EMG. Later Tommy learned the results.

"It's nerve damage, Tommy. Something in the elbow is cutting off one of the nerves. I'll send a report to Doctor Stark and to Doctor Jobe."

"Is that why my fingers are stiff and don't move right?" Tommy asked.

The doctor nodded.

After additional examinations Dr. Jobe and Dr. Stark told Tommy they would have to inspect the nerve to find out why it wasn't working as it should. The third operation on Tommy's pitching arm was done December 17, 1974. During the operation the surgeons found that scar tissue had formed and was surrounding part of the nerve, thus blocking its function.

They decided to lift the nerve from its channel (running through the back of the arm and elbow) and after removing the scar tissue, repositioned it deep inside the muscle tissue at and below the elbow.

"You'll be the only kid on the block with your 'crazy bone' on your forearm," joked Dr. Jobe. No one really knew what to expect, if anything, as a result of the two operations.

As Tommy recuperated from the latest arm operation, the number of get-well cards and notes increased—and were encouraging. He especially appreciated one such greeting. It came in an envelope with WHITE HOUSE as the return address. Inside was a brief hand-written note from President Gerald Ford:

> Dear Tommy,
> I hope that your arm operation is successful You were doing great in '74 until that unfortunate incident. I do keep track of you. I'll see you soon.
> JERRY FORD

Tommy and Sally, along with three-month-old Tami, flew to Indiana to share the Christmas holidays with their parents—and new grandparents. Their happiness was severely dampened as they all watched Tommy's shriveled hand. Tommy was self-conscious because of their pity and a cloud of depression hung over their holidays. The busy time, however, kept their minds off the problem.

In January, Tommy felt badly that he'd be unable to play in the Bing Crosby Pro-Am golf tournament at Pebble Beach, but gripping a golf club was by now out of the question.

Sally began to get a feeling of panic. She never expressed anything but optimism and hopefulness to Tommy. But deep inside, she was troubled. Doctor Jobe had shared only with her his fear that Tommy could never pitch again. "You'd better encourage him to find a new line of work just in case. The Dodgers will carry him on the disabled list until his contract expires, so he's got a year to find something. There's no hurry—but get him started thinking about something besides baseball for a career."

Sally could not bring herself to share this bad news bluntly with Tommy. During their prayer times together, they sought God's peace and some kind of understanding for what had happened to Tommy.

There were still times when bitterness and anger at God overwhelmed her, but for the most part, Sally was helped by Tommy's quiet assurance.

After six weeks, the cast was removed from Tommy's pitching arm. The arm had atrophied badly. The muscle in his forearm and hand looked like a deflated balloon. Skin hung loosely around his arm. Bony fingers were skeletal and his skin was dry and peeling.

Sally's eyes filled with tears and she looked away as she and Tommy tried to massage life and feeling back into the arm and hand. His fingers were curled grotesquely and hooklike at the end of his hand. But it was time to rebuild and think positively of the day he could pitch.

About this time, Tommy received copies of a new baseball contract in the mail. The terms called for the same financial arrangements as the previous contract.

"I'm disappointed," Tommy told attorney Bob Cohen. "I thought they'd offer an increase because of my record last season. I think I contributed to the Dodgers winning the pennant.''

"I do, too,'' explained Bob. "But you have to see it from the Dodgers' point of view, too. I'm sure they think they're being extra charitable to even offer you a contract when you're disabled. They have to look at the cold fact that maybe . . . ."

"That maybe I'll never pitch again?''

"Uh . . . yeah . . . I'm sure they've thought of it.''

"But I will pitch again, Bob.''

"Sure you will, Tommy,'' the attorney replied. "But meanwhile, let's think of ways to negotiate with the club.'' Usually negotiations are based on contributions of the year before. But not this time. Last year meant nothing at contract time.

Tommy held out for a better contract. The ball club, with no real assurance that Tommy would ever be anything other than a disabled pitcher, refused to offer more. Tommy decided not to sign and the contract was still unsigned by spring-training time.

The baseball contracts have a standard renewal clause which gives the ball club the right to renew the contract for one year at any salary so long as the cut, if there is to be one, does not exceed 20 percent of the previous year's salary.

"The Dodgers will probably invoke the renewal clause in early March,'' Bob Cohen told Tommy.

Tommy and Sally had stopped off in Phoenix to visit Sally's aunt and uncle, then continued on their way to Florida and spring training.

Just outside El Paso, Tommy noticed Sally was preoccupied. She was concerned about her mother, recovering from an operation in an Indiana hospital. "Would you like to go and see your mom before we go to spring training?''

"Now? But it's already February twenty-fourth and you have to report . . . .''

"I don't have a contract yet. Besides I can't pitch, so let's visit your mom until we hear from the club.''

On March 8, Tommy received a special-delivery letter from the Dodgers. He fumbled with the envelope, his withered hand gave him no help.

"Here," he said to Sally finally, "you open it."

She tore the envelope and took out the letter for him.

"It says they are invoking the renewal clause . . . and renewing my contract . . . ."

"With a twenty percent salary cut?" asked Sally.

"No . . . the same terms as last year," he grinned. "Maybe it's the Dodgers' way of saying they still want me. I was talking to a Cincinnati pitcher who was sidelined for two years. I asked him what the Reds offered him and he said they gave him a twenty percent cut. This *is* pretty nice of the club. Yessir, the Dodgers are a first-class organization. You really feel like playing baseball when they treat you so well."

"Then you're going to sign?"

"I'm still going to push for a raise," Tommy replied, "on the basis of my record—what I did toward the Dodgers' season success. I feel I helped them get to the first hurdles, the play-offs, and I should be compensated, however small it is."

From Florida Tommy and Sally called Bob Cohen in Los Angeles and asked him if he would be willing to get in touch with Al Campanis and negotiate at least a token raise in light of T.J.'s fine record the previous year—a record which in part contributed to the Dodgers' winning their division and subsequently getting into the World Series. Bob talked to both Al and Peter O'Malley, and discussed, among other things, why the raise was important to Tommy. The Dodgers finally consented to give a three-thousand-dollar raise, even though they knew he would not be able to pitch that year.

Tommy put himself into the grueling physical pace of typical spring training. He dressed and exercised as if he were going to pitch in the regular rotation. He could move his arm and go through the pitching motion, but the scar tissue by cutting off the nerve had already done its damage. Tommy could only throw a ball by placing it in his pitching hand and pulling the fingers over the ball with his other hand. There was no feeling, movement, or control in the fingers of his left hand, so his efforts were futile. He could actually throw the ball this way, but it was not a pitch. And to Tommy's way of thinking, it was a waste of a catcher's time to work out with him.

Tommy practiced by himself in spring training by throwing the ball against a cement wall. His first efforts were clumsy little dribblers that only went thirty feet. With effort and concentration, he managed to make the ball go forty, sometimes fifty feet.

He worked on his fielding too, but couldn't throw, so as a result he was terribly ineffective.

Unable to play, Tommy nonetheless felt an obligation to the club to justify his salary and raise obtained that spring. He went to see Peter O'Malley one day to discuss his feelings.

"You're paying me a very good salary and I'd like to do something to earn it," Tommy said.

"Well, maybe if . . . uh . . . *when* you get your arm back," O'Malley replied gently.

"No, I mean now."

"What do you have in mind?"

"Well, Peter," Tommy answered, "I would like to chart pitches of the other teams. I can clock their pitching speed with the radar gun—maybe even take some movies. We can look at their offensive tendencies and give our players some ideas for defensive positions. I could make charts of how the other guys pitch to us and give them to the coaches."

"That sounds great. You can begin at once," O'Malley said.

Tommy felt he was making a contribution, of course, but deep inside there was a painful emotional strain to be present and watch his teammates play—and then have to sit in the stands by himself. He became very frustrated having to sit out games. Driving to the ball park with Joe Ferguson, Tom Paciorek and the then third base coach Tommy Lasorda often led to conversations of how to play Johnny Bench or Joe Morgan or pitch to George Foster. Tommy participated in the discussions but agonized inside when the others took to the field, and he had to be on the sidelines.

In Los Angeles, during batting practice, Tommy was tougher on himself than ever before. He ran farther than before, did more knee bends, exercised longer and harder, lifted more weights than he ever had before.

He tried to pitch using his unorthodox "grip"—that of forcing two fingers to hold the ball by curling the paralyzed fingers alongside the seams with his good hand. He even tried taping his left hand so the fingers would not uncurl on their own, making him drop the ball before it could be thrown.

Yet, as hard as he worked, futility dogged him at every new effort.

Rod Dedeaux, baseball coach at the University of Southern California, is a close personal friend of Tommy. Rod saw Tommy often during what he felt were hopeless workouts. He never told Tommy, of course, not wanting to diminish Tommy's hopes, but he was convinced the Dodger pitcher was wasting his time.

"The odds are just too great," Rod told himself. As a baseball coach, he knew what an injury like this would do to a man's arm. "No, Tommy can never come back. It's just too impractical, illogical."

Rod admired Tommy's mental attitude, however. "When Tommy is finally ready to admit defeat," Rod told himself, "I'll talk to him about coaching. He has an exceptional ability to communicate to players—he will make an ideal coach when his playing days are over. And barring some kind of miracle, that's where Tommy is right now."

Red Adams, the Dodger pitching coach, ached inside as he watched his one-time pitching great reduced to a one-armed statistician. *Who is he kidding?* Red asked himself one day. *He'll never pitch again and the sooner he realizes it the better off he'll be. Why doesn't somebody tell him?* But even in the asking, Red knew no one who *would* tell Tommy.

"The guy should be realistic," Tommy overheard one of his teammates say one day. "I mean, what's he trying to prove? He's finished. Why doesn't he face up to it?"

Red didn't know whether to encourage Tommy to keep trying or face the reality of his handicap. He decided it was up to someone else to discourage him. He continued to help Tommy as best he could. Red worked with the crippled pitcher to rig up a harness of straps and tape that would help his paralyzed fingers grip the ball. But it all seemed so useless.

Sally struggled alone with the knowledge that, as far as Dr. Jobe could tell, it appeared doubtful Tommy would ever pitch again. Yet she still could not bring herself to completely cripple Tommy's hopes as well as his arm. She felt Tommy knew his own body and its limitations. She did not have to say anything, however. Tommy knew her thoughts. He was also sensitive enough to know the fears and uncertainties of Dr. Jobe after visiting him weekly for nearly four months now.

Tommy didn't expect any encouragement from the ball club or players. The club had to deal with facts, harsh though they might be. And the players were part of an overall competitive structure where it might even be in their best interest if Tommy *was* washed up. It would mean, for several pitchers below Tommy on the minor league level, a move up the ladder by one rung.

Tommy was most frustrated, however, by simple things over which he no longer had control. Forks of food dropped from his hand and he had to teach himself how to eat with his right hand. He had to find a different way to brush his hair. The bank called to check on his signature because they could not decipher his scrawl.

The first game of golf he tried to play with his crippled hand was a long, long day. Normally a high 70 or low 80 shooter (10 handicap), Tommy had to sink a 15-foot putt to break 100. "That was the longest hardest round of golf I have ever played," said Tommy. "Now I know what a 20–24 handicapper goes through." But it was a happy round of golf too, because now he had a goal to shoot for. Now he could go forward and keep on working for lower scores.

His thoughts and prayers were a jumble. Then a quiet peace settled over him. It was as if Tommy's prayer was heard and God was saying to him: *Tommy, I gave you the gift to pitch. I can take it away. It isn't the gift that's important—it's you. You are My child. This experience is for your good. I've allowed it to happen. Perhaps you don't understand just now, but trust Me.*

But, Lord, baseball is what I love. How can I have a crippled arm and still play? I can't believe You want me to give up baseball, Tommy argued with God.

Trust Me. Give all your worries to Me. I always return more than is taken. This tragedy will be a blessing. You will see.

Tommy determined to trust God. "If not baseball, then something better," he reasoned.

Sally tried to share his confidence, but her faith was not as strong as his. Her heart ached at the sight of his withered arm and hooked fingers. She grieved as he constantly pulled and stretched his unfeeling fingers, trying to stimulate muscle growth and tone. She was constantly worrying if Tommy was adjusting to the idea that his baseball career was probably over.

10

"For With God Nothing Shall Be Impossible"

Tommy began to wonder how Jesus had mastered difficulty and defeat. As he read through various passages in the Bible in which Christ had faced problems, he saw that Christ did so through prayer. Tommy and Sally followed that pattern. This was the most difficult time of their lives together—yet instead of the circumstances driving them apart, their love and relationship were made stronger.

One Sunday morning they were in church and Lareau was preaching.

"My text this morning," Pastor Lareau began, "is Luke 1:37: 'For with God nothing shall be impossible.' "

As he began his sermon, Lareau explained that the theme of his message was the power of God.

"God's power is remarkable and makes men's efforts puny in comparison," Lareau told his congregation. "We here in Southern California know a little of God's power through what happened here five years ago. On February ninth, 1971, an earthquake shook the valley and terrified hundreds, perhaps thousands. Thankfully, it did not cause widespread loss of life. Despite modern man's ingenuity, power, and ability, there was absolutely nothing he could do to prevent God from shaking the earth."

As Lareau continued, Tommy and Sally both listened with interest as he outlined from the Scriptures displays of God's power—in Creation, in nature, finally explaining the greatest display of God's power.

"Without a doubt the Resurrection of Jesus Christ from the dead is God's greatest demonstration of His power. And the Bible says, in Ephesians 1:19, 20, that this same power which God used to raise Christ from the dead, He longs to unleash in our lives today. That same mighty, miraculous power—the Bible says—is available to us who believe in Him."

Lareau paused to let his words register, then continued. "God's power can forgive sin. God's power can make your life a witness for Him."

Picking up his Bible from the pulpit, Lareau held it up for emphasis. "God's Word says that His power can give you victory over temptation. God's power," he said, "can help you face affliction with power."

Tommy looked down at his Bible. He took out a pen and underlined the words from Luke's Gospel: *For with God nothing shall be impossible.*

Lord, Tommy prayed, *is this true?* He looked up from his Bible to see Lareau's piercing eyes fixed directly on him.

"God's power," Lareau seemed to say directly to Tommy, "can work a *miracle* in your life—right now!"

Lareau had no way of knowing that Tommy would be in the congregation that morning, of course. His message was developed to be addressed to all who heard. But Tommy felt it had been prepared specifically for him. It seemed Lareau was still looking directly into his eyes and addressing his words only to him.

"Some of you in the sanctuary this morning are facing impossible situations by human definitions."

Tommy listened carefully as Lareau continued.

"I believe God would like to display His power in *your* life this morning. You're facing odds and obstacles that are impossible, but God says, 'Let Me demonstrate My power in your situation.' You know that there is absolutely no way out for you unless God performs a miracle."

A miracle? Tommy turned the idea over in his mind. He squeezed Sally's hand. She returned the pressure to communicate that her thoughts were running parallel to his own. Tears of hope and happiness welled up in her eyes.

"God wants us to get to the place where we *trust Him,*" Lareau added. It was the same thought that God seemed to give to Tommy earlier.

"In Genesis eighteen, Abraham—over a hundred years old—tells his wife, Sarah, some eighty years old, that God promised them a child. Think of the impossibility of that situation. What a cruel hoax—a *baby*— at their age? But God promised—and Abraham says to Sarah, in verse fourteen, 'Is anything too hard for the Lord?'

"You see," Lareau continued, "that's the only qualification you need. No matter what you need—how impossible your situation. Ask yourself: 'Is anything too hard for God?' "

God brought life and healing to withered, paralyzed limbs, Tommy knew. The Bible told of many such instances. *But that was two thousand years ago,* Tommy told himself. *What about today? What about me?*

God seemed to be conversing directly with Tommy through his thoughts and Lareau's preaching. "Right now," Lareau said with conviction and authority, "I believe it's *you* that God is talking to. He has His mighty power. You have an impossible situation. You need nothing short of a miracle—and that's exactly what He wants to do in your life. Why don't you let Him work His power in you?"

Tommy was deeply moved and had never felt such power and conviction at work in his life before. In the closing prayer of commitment, Tommy gave his handicap to God with a silent prayer of expectancy. "Lord, I'm going to take You at Your Word. You've said that nothing is impossible for You. And you say in the Bible that if we ask anything in Your name, it will be given. I pray for completeness—for healing and restoration. If You'll do Your part— I'll do mine. I'll work and trust Your power, because I believe that such a thing is completely possible."

Tommy took the Word seriously and began to focus his thoughts on the goal of complete restoration of his arm and hand. Nothing short of complete recovery was enough. His goal was—humanly speaking—all but impossible. But, as he reminded himself regularly from the underlined verse in his Bible, "For nothing is impossible with the Lord."

Tommy and Sally found more and more strength from church and their friends from church and their neighborhood. Indeed, those who seemed to be closest to Tommy and Sally during their ordeal *were* those from their church and neighborhood. They stopped by with a word of encouragement or casserole when Sally had the flu. Or they'd phone to encourage Tommy and remind him, "We're praying for you."

Evie and Lareau Lindquist became two of their closest confidants. Evie was the type of friend Sally could open her heart to and receive understanding and strength in return. Tommy was also growing in his faith and spiritual understanding under Lareau's leadership.

Evie taught a ladies' Bible class and invited Sally. She joined and with the class began to study the writings of Saint Paul. Sally shared her insights with Tommy.

"Listen," she told him, "we can accomplish anything through Christ's power."

"Where does it say that in the Bible?"

"Right here," she said, thumbing through the Living Bible, "Philippians 4:13, 'I can do all things through Christ who gives me the strength and power.' "

Humanly speaking, it was the lowest point in their lives. Promises from the Bible—hope—it all seemed far away, remote. Yet, the promises were all they had. (Bible passages which encouraged Tommy and Sally during this troubling time included: Philippians 3:13, 14; 1 Thessalonians 5:16–18; Mark 9:23; Romans 5:5–10; and James 1:1–6.)

Tommy had learned the realities of life through the conditioning of being a major league ballplayer. So many capricious elements can make or break a career, so he learned early how to roll with life's punches.

When a few former acquaintances had forsaken them, Sally was crushed. Tommy, however, explained how the competitive nature of sports sometimes limits friendships to only a surface level.

It seems Tami could not have arrived at a better time, either. They were blessed with a beautiful baby whom Tommy would hold, inspiring and uplifting his spirits again and again. "For you, Sweetheart," he seemed to be saying to her, "I'll make it . . . for *you*."

However, Tommy knew it would take more than faith in God and himself. He did not expect a sudden supernatural healing. Rather, he was convinced that God would use natural means to give him back his arm.

Others were not as convinced as Tommy. Two Dodger trainers, Jack Homel and Bill Buhler, were among the handful that did believe Tommy. Like Ben Wade, Tom Lasorda and Sally, they believed Tommy would succeed because *he* told them he would. Tommy seemed to have enough faith for them all.

Jack Homel was a champion wrist wrestler and held a world title for twenty years. His strong arm and hand muscles were almost gifted as he worked as the Dodgers' masseur. Jack spent countless hours working of Tommy's forearm, shoulder, and hand, giving special attention to his fingers—pulling, stretching, rubbing, trying to get more circulation in the fingers. Bill Buhler, the other trainer, was the "Edison" of the trainers. He was always inventing gadgets for the players to use to improve their muscular control or ability.

In Montreal one day, Tommy was walking down the street with Bill and spotted something unusual in a sporting goods display.

"What's that thing, Bill?"

"It's a karate 'crusher'," Bill answered as Tommy looked closely at the device. It was circular ring with five springs attached. Small rings were fastened to the springs.

"The idea," continued Bill, "is for a guy who's into karate to build up his hand muscles by putting his fingers into the small rings and pulling on the strings, stretching the finger muscles. Supposed to give a guy a grip of steel."

"I think I ought to buy one and try it with my left hand," Tommy commented.

"No . . . the springs are too tight. You have to start with something less resistant. Let me see what I can do." Bill's inventive mind was already at work.

Back in Los Angeles, it was only a couple of days later that Bill offered Tommy a variation of the karate crusher. He used a utensil from the housewares department of a nearby department store.

"That's a ring like Sally uses to cool cakes when she takes them out of the oven," Tommy remarked.

"Right," Bill said. "Now the idea is to take this rubber band and use your finger to fasten it to the ring. See how you have to stretch your fingers?"

Tommy saw how easily Bill demonstrated the device. He tried it, but his stiff fingers would not respond without determined effort. Finally, he was able to force one rubber band on the ring.

Jack and Bill worked with Tommy in the trainer's room. He ran nearly ten miles every day, spent time in the whirlpool bath and ultra-sound treatment, hoping that more blood would circulate through his arms and fingers.

Tommy combined three "eggs" of Silly Putty and exercised for hours by squeezing it in his hand, alternating that with the rubber-band ring. He even carried Silly Putty in his glove compartment and squeezed it during drives to the ball park. Still there was no measurable improvement.

"That's all right, Tommy," Dr. Jobe told him one day. "Keep it up. It'll keep you in shape. You never know about nerve damage. It may be permanent, but even if it isn't, it'll take months—maybe years—before it heals. Nerves regenerate about an inch per month. Your nerves were pinched off at the elbow. That means you have about a foot and a half of nerve to be restored. That's expecting an awful lot," he said quietly, but then added, "that is, expecting a lot in a short time. Also, we don't know how the period of inactivity will affect the muscles."

Watching Tommy inflict himself with such a torturous routine was an emotional struggle for Sally. Outwardly she encouraged Tommy, cheered every small success. But inside, her feelings of pity and doubt were nearly unbearable.

One evening the two of them went over to have dinner with Evie and Lareau. After dinner Tommy methodically squeezed and stretched with the wire and rubber ring. When he excused himself to go to the bathroom, Sally broke down.

"Oh, Evie," she cried, "I can't take it any longer. My heart breaks when I see what he's putting himself through!''

Sally unburdened herself on Evie's shoulder. ''You two are the only ones I've felt free to share my feelings with. I'm scared. I'm afraid Tommy won't be able to play baseball again. I know God will take care of us—but Tommy believes so much that God is going to give him a miracle, I can't show him how I really feel—that I'm scared. That I have doubts—that maybe he's expecting the impossible.''

''Sally,'' comforted Lareau, ''don't worry about Tommy. He's at a low point in his life physically, but I've never seen him more fit spiritually. God is somehow using this experience to enrich his life and character. All we can do is stand back and be supportive . . . let Tommy know we love him and want—just as he does—God's best for him.''

''Well, Tommy *has* helped me spiritually,'' Sally admitted. ''He's so strong in his faith and with the Lord.''

''Then look for how God will use this experience,'' Lareau advised. ''I know already that you two have never been closer. That's something to be thankful for. And Tami . . . and all the things you have as a family, spiritually. Remember, Jesus told His followers to take one day at a time—that one day's trouble is enough for one day.''

''Now you sound like Tommy,'' Sally sniffed, smiling.

''It's good advice, Sally. Trust God . . . and take each day at a time. Don't worry about tomorrow, about next season, about five years from now. Let God take care of those concerns,'' Evie added.

Sally nodded and wiped her eyes as Lareau continued.

''Tommy told me about a book he's just read by Wes Neal—something about athletic perfection coupled with spiritual growth. I think the idea is to try and conform our lives more to the image and character of Christ. And that's never easy.''

It would not be easy for either of them. Tommy persisted with the agony of rehabilitation, until even he was nearly convinced of its hopelessness. But every time he became discouraged, he reminded himself of God's promises.

Tommy was working in the grandstand, clocking the speed of

pitches with a radar gun and charting their various pitches. Many times he would talk almost like a coach, and he was genuinely interested in what the team was doing.

Sally also felt on the outside, looking in. She sat in the stands with the other players' wives, but it seemed difficult for the other wives to find something to talk about. Increasingly she felt shut out of what was happening with the Dodgers and "the Dodger family." After a while, she went to fewer and fewer games. More and more she was hurt by what she felt was the lack of interest and concern. Consequently, Sally spent a great deal more time on the phone with Evie, who encouraged her through her interest and prayer support. She also depended on the shoulders of a couple of neighbors at this time.

One day Sally was next door visiting Lil Varvello and burst into tears. "Tommy just called himself a cripple. He said it as a joke, but I know he meant it!" she sobbed.

"Sally," consoled Lil, "please . . . just have faith. It will be all right." Lil and Ed had a son Tommy's age, so felt parental instincts to give their young neighbors help and encouragement.

Bob and Beth Allsup, also neighbors, had children Tommy's and Sally's ages and considered themselves their "adopted" parents. When she was pregnant with Tami, Sally had often asked Beth for advice.

Other times Sally would be a bit frightened or "weepy" as she shared her fears with Beth or Lil, but always regained her composure before seeing Tommy. She was always strong when around him, or at ball games, for his sake.

It was great to have close friends as neighbors. Since Tommy was gone a lot, that left a lot of time for Sally to be alone. Just talking about your feelings certainly helped, Sally recalls.

Friends from the Yorba Linda Free Church and other neighbors were supportive. It was more than encouragement. These folks shared their hurts and hopes. They had become Tommy and Sally's new "family."

"We hated to burden our families with our sad feelings. They were so far away and our calls would only depress them," Sally recalls.

As they learned about the daily life experiences of their friends, Tommy and Sally discovered that they also had their own troubles and concerns. As couples got together for times of sharing and mutual support, they would invariably end with a time of prayer—asking God for the strength to cope.

Tommy's routine with the Dodgers continued to be one of grueling physical workouts and charting of pitches during the games. Tommy could have worked out at the nearby YMCA and thrown balls at the fence in his backyard. But he chose to stay with the team, as difficult—emotionally—as this might be.

"I feel I owe the players, the Dodgers, and the Los Angeles fans that much," he explained one day. "These guys are the greatest group I have ever played with. I have to try and come back for them."

Six months had gone by since his second arm operation. Still there was no progress in the recovery of his hand. The exercises and massaging by Tommy and Dodger trainers had built the muscles back to just under their former size. The hand no longer appeared to be atrophied, yet it was still paralyzed and numb. Tommy's fingers were cold, stiff, and curled. The hand resembled a monkey's hand more than a man's hand. His fingers had only a remote sensation of touch, a feeling as if they were "asleep." The slow recovery time was very frustrating. Each morning Tommy and Sally would awaken, hoping his nerve condition had improved.

The months of therapy and exercising his hand enabled Tommy to begin to throw the ball again. He still had to place his fingers around the ball with his other hand, but could throw the baseball pretty well even with the unorthodox grip.

On a road trip to Chicago in June, he decided to throw batting practice at Wrigley Field. It really wasn't an outstanding job, but he did put the ball over the plate with a degree of professionalism. As he continued, players from the Dodgers and Cubs walked up to the screen behind home plate to watch.

The Dodgers, of course, had watched Tommy with some degree of interest and saw his determination. The Cubs knew only of the injury and heard the secondhand stories of Tommy's faith in a comeback.

"Hey, that's pretty good!" called out one of the Dodger infielders.

"Compared to what?" Tommy cracked. "Compared to Tommy John six months ago?"

But it *was* good. Not good enough to pitch in games against major league hitters again, but good enough for batting practice.

On a road trip to Pittsburgh a week later, Tommy learned a trick of putting his thumb on the ball a bit differently. By taking the numb fingers and curling them along the seams, then taking his thumb and pushing it against the side of the ball, Tommy discovered that he could throw a fast ball that actually had a little of the old "pop" on it, one of the first signs of a good fast ball. He was really excited and the will to succeed kept him going.

He pitched like that in daily batting practice for about a month. His pitches were getting better, although still far from having the qualities he had had before—and to be the pitcher the Dodgers needed.

As he began to work harder on his pitching, Coach Red Adams played an important role. He watched Tommy in the bull pen, frequently acting as Tommy's catcher. He checked Tommy's pitching mechanics to be sure his pitcher had not picked up any bad habits during his long hiatus. Tommy was just trying to regain that "old sinker ball" that had been his "bread-and-butter" pitch, and which had made him the leading pitcher in the National League in July of '74. Al Campanis, the Dodger Vice-President of Player Personnel, watched Tommy working out. He knew a difficult decision would have to be made soon. Should the Dodgers carry Tommy another year on the disabled list or release him? Campanis wondered if it was wishful thinking on Tommy's part—and his part, too—that he would regain his pitching ability. Campanis would surely get criticism for carrying Tommy much longer—like the criticism he got when he made the deal to trade Richie Allen to the White Sox for Tommy earlier.

Campanis watched Tommy desperately trying to throw the ball and felt an ache inside. He remembered scouting Tommy, then a White Sox pitcher, during games at Angel Stadium in Anaheim, just a few miles from Campanis's home. He liked the style and ability of this left-handed pitcher. Al grinned, recalling that the Angel batters had only hit four balls to the outfield off Tommy in that 9-inning game, but poor fielding lost the game for him. Yet, Campanis knew Tommy, even in losing, was good. He had proceeded with his plans to trade Allen for Tommy.

Ruefully, Campanis now recalled that his protégé was on his way to his greatest season ever in the major leagues when the arm injury sidelined him. Now? Well, there would be a decision to make soon enough.

During that interval, however, a curious thing began to happen. It seemed to Tommy that he was getting feeling back in his little finger. A few days later, he thought feeling was slowly returning to his other fingers, then his thumb.

He didn't say anything to Sally, however, because the paralysis was still there. Even if the sense of feeling did return—not knowing the extent or nature of the nerve damage—it would be impossible to know whether he would ever overcome the paralysis.

. . . *with God nothing shall be impossible.* Tommy grabbed at the words every time they came to his consciousness and clung to the promises the verse implied.

By the July All-Star break, it was obvious that feeling *was* returning to his fingers. Tommy came home to tell Sally, but by the time he got there, the surprise was even sweeter.

"Close your eyes," he told her when he came in the door.

She did as he asked. "What is it?"

"Okay . . . you can open them now."

Sally blinked.

"Now watch," he said. With extreme concentration and willpower, he looked with intensity at his hand. Then slowly, almost imperceptibly, he straightened his little finger.

"Tommy!" Sally shrieked. "You did it! The nerve is coming back!"

He wiggled the little finger slowly, curling and uncurling it on command, the first time it responded to the brain's impulses since the operation on September 25, 1974.

The two of them were ecstatic because of what this meant. They embraced, cried, and jumped around the kitchen with excitement.

"Oh, thank You, God!" cried Sally. "Thank You, thank You, *thank* You!"

Later that night they talked about it in more subdued ways.

"Do you know what this means?" laughed Tommy. "I'll be able to pitch by next season. I can *pitch* again! Not just throw batting practice—*pitch!* The nerve is coming back—now all I have to do is build up the muscles."

"It means there's hope, Tommy," said Sally. "I prayed that you'd get back the use of your hands and fingers. I didn't want to be greedy and ask for more."

"Well, I know that I'm not ready to pitch yet. But I will be. It may be that God will only give me back my hands and fingers but not the ability to pitch. He may not plan for me to be able to pitch again, but I'm going to give it one heck of a battle!" Tommy said emphatically.

John Wooden, the great UCLA basketball coach, had told Tommy that summer, "You'll gain strength through adversity. You'll be a stronger person and a better Christian from this experience." Tommy now remembered his words and knew what was meant by them.

For the next two months Tommy threw batting practice every day, building and strengthening crucial muscles. By September Tommy's fingers were responding quite well to the motor impulses of his brain. He felt it was time to put his efforts to the test. The Dodgers were ten games behind and there was no way for them to get into the play-offs by the end of the month, so Tommy felt he could ask Al Campanis for a favor.

"Al, could you get me into the Instructional League?" he requested.

There was genuine interest in the eyes of the Dodger Vice-President. "You mean you're ready to test the arm against hitters?"

Tommy nodded.

"Well, sure. I'll let you off. Can you be ready to go to Phoenix by the twenty-fifth?"

"I'm ready right now."

"Great. I'll set it up."

Tommy, Sally, and Tami drove to Phoenix from Los Angeles that last week in September. They moved into an apartment and Tommy began to work out with the team.

The Instructional League consisted of outstanding young ballplayers just signed out of high school and college. It was a place for them to get the necessary professional experience in a controlled situation. They were minor league players but quality hitters.

Tommy pitched his first game on Monday, September 29. Sally took Tami with her to the park to watch. Al Campanis came by and waved at Sally. She called out to him.

"Doesn't Tommy look beautiful out there in his Dodger uniform on the mound?"

Al winked at her. "Yeah . . . he looks great. He's going to be okay, Sally. He'll do fine." Al then went to watch the game more closely with other Dodger officials.

Lord, Sally prayed at the start of the game, *I'm thankful . . . but please be with Tommy and give him the strength to be able to pitch effectively.*

On the mound, Tommy's thoughts were also prayerful.

Lord, just help me do the best I can.

Tommy looked at the plate from the pitcher's mound. Catcher Kevin Pasley had been brought down by the Dodgers to catch for Tommy. There was no misunderstanding of the importance of this opportunity. Tommy knew he had to impress the Dodger management people who were watching this game.

"Play ball!" called the umpire as he ceremoniously broomed home plate for the first California Angel rookie batter.

It was now one year—almost to the day—since Tommy's first arm operation. It had been a year and a half since Tommy was on the mound pitching in a real game and not routine batting practice.

There was expectancy inside the ball park, as players and fans waited for Tommy John's comeback attempt.

Tommy went into the pitching motion and wound up. The batter tensed, and stiffened, the bat poised over his shoulder. The pitch was released. It sailed toward the plate, but was high. The batter relaxed, and Kevin had to jump up to catch it.

"Ball one!" called the umpire.

The batter tapped his shoe with the bat and nervously dug his front foot into the loose dirt, once again taking his stance.

Tommy again wound up to pitch. Again the ball nearly sailed past the catcher, outside, and quite high over the plate.

"Ball two!"

Sally, sitting in the stands, bit her lip, and blinked back tears.

Al Campanis and other Dodger management people and coaches sat quietly near the dugout. No one spoke, yet the thought was on everyone's mind. *He's lost it!*

On the mound Tommy caught the ball from Kevin and took off his glove to roll it around in his two hands. Then, concentrating on the batter, he put the glove back on and stepped to the mound. He remembered that during his rehabilitation he'd held the ball with his fingers some two inches apart instead of the old closed-finger grip he had learned. It was obvious that until he could regain the unconscious mechanics of pitching as before, he would have to rehearse each pitch carefully.

Tommy placed the ball in his pitching hand, conscious of *how* he was holding it. He went into his motion, again calling upon his memory to define the exact movements of that routine. Instinctively, Tommy felt this was better.

"Strike one!" yelled the umpire as a curve ball whizzed over the plate to *"whap"* into Kevin's glove with the old power and authority.

Tommy grinned.

Sally cheered and hugged Tami.

Al Campanis looked at a Dodger coach and nodded.

Tommy's next pitch was a fast ball. The Angel batter swung at it and grounded out.

The next batter also grounded out. The next one struck out.

Tommy was scheduled to pitch 3 innings so as not to strain his arm. The 3 innings went by so quickly, Sally was amazed. He had pitched 3 innings of no-hit baseball, gave up no walks, and struck out 4 batters.

It was a joyous, bubbling Tommy John who returned to the Dodger dugout after his debut. But the word was out by now, and before Tommy had showered and dressed, the clubhouse telephone was ringing constantly as sportswriters across the country called to ask how Tommy did and to get his response.

It was a happy, exciting time. Sally called her parents and Tommy's folks, nearly shouting the good news into the telephone. "Three innings . . . and no hits, no walks! And Al Campanis saw it all!" Tommy was so exhilarated he could hardly sleep that night. Sally was happy for him and the two of them talked of the future.

"One day at a time, you said," reminded Sally. "Let's think one day at a time."

"Yes! The next game is against San Diego. I'll try and pitch 5 innings."

The game against San Diego was sparked by 5 innings of Tommy's superb shutout pitching. In the next game, against the Cubs, Tommy asked to stay in for 6 innings. He gave up only 1 run during those 6 innings.

After a little more than a month of Instructional League play, Tommy's record was 3–1. He was pitching and pitching effectively.

Going back to Los Angeles in November, Tommy and Sally talked about all that had happened since his injury.

"I never took anything for granted," Sally confessed. "I prayed that you'd get your hand back. But, as far as pitching—well, that's frosting on the cake."

"All the little things seem to have had a purpose," Tommy mused. "If the nerve hadn't healed so slowly, who knows—maybe I'd have come back too soon and damaged my arm permanently. Mike Marshall told me it was a blessing in disguise.

"Well," Tommy said after a long silence, "Lareau was right." He looked ahead as they drove and his mind was deep in thought. "Nothing is impossible with God. Like it says in Mark 9:23, 'Anything is possible if you have faith.' That's the key word. *Faith.*"

Tommy knew he still had a big hill to climb. There is a tremendous difference between minor league and major league hitters, but at least he was prepared to give it all he had.

11

Comeback

After Christmas it was time to begin preparing for the 1976 season. At no other time in Tommy's career had he been so eager to get started. All winter he and Sally played catch by the hour in their backyard, as Tommy worked toward making his comeback. He began to exercise in January, and was running between five and ten miles a day by the time he was to report to spring training.

The Dodgers had sent Tommy another one-year contract at the same salary. He decided to use Bob Cohen to directly represent him in contract talks with the Dodgers; that way Tommy could devote his full time to playing ball.

"They're offering me the same contract as last year, and that's fine with me," said Tommy.

Bob thumbed through the pages. "The same as last year?" he repeated. "But last year you only pitched four games of minor league ball. You'll do much better this year."

"Yes, but I have to prove myself to them."

"Well, the whole idea of negotiating is to end up with a contract that is fair to both sides. Yours is fair, until you prove you can make a comeback. But there's nothing here for you if you have a really impressive year for the Dodgers. Al Campanis suggests that you accept the contract as it stands, but work out a salary increase system for every game you start. It's fair to the Dodgers because they aren't going to start you if you aren't producing—and it's fair to you because if you make the requisite number of starts, you will receive a salary commensurate with what you would have received had you not been injured and unable to pitch."

Al Campanis and Bob Cohen discussed the idea of a contract based on performance and agreed it was fair to both parties. If Tommy started in 20 games during the 1976 season, he'd earn a substantial salary increase. If he started in 30 games, the increase would be even greater. Al Campanis realized the unique nature of the situation: that Tommy, not having pitched, was worth so much money—but if he was able to pitch, would be worth an additional sum of money. Al had the flexibility and foresight to consent to the increase. Tommy signed the contract and began to concentrate on earning his salary.

Spring training was delayed in 1976 because of a dispute between the major league Baseball Players Association and the club owners. For nearly three weeks the players were "locked out" and spring training postponed.

Tommy personally wished the dispute had been settled quickly. He needed pitching experience to get back the rhythm of the game and recover the feelings, the mechanics—those important intangibles. He needed the experience, the regular pitching rotation to get back into the routine. After all, he had not pitched since July of 1974 in a major league game.

When spring training finally got under way, Tommy tried to make use of every available moment to make up for lost time. He worked out earlier and longer than anyone else on the team. He knew he had a tremendous job of rebuilding to recover the speed, accuracy, and power that his arm had provided him before the injury.

Then, of course, there were the inevitable questions. He remembered when he had had bone-chip surgery—how reporters, teammates, coaches, and fans alike all put his arm under magnified scrutiny, wondering if he'd regain the prowess he had before. Only now there seemed to be good cause to question his arm.

The first spring-training game Tommy pitched was against the Mets in Saint Petersburg. Tommy pitched 4 innings and had a very good outing. The pitches were getting better, the control sharper, and the confidence returning. The second game was against the Baltimore Orioles in Vero Beach. Tommy pitched 6 innings in that game and struck out 6 Oriole batters, but Walt Alston decided

Tommy's arm was questionable.

"You're not throwing the ball hard enough," the manager told him. "You've just got to throw it harder."

The radar gun had timed Tommy at a speed of 80 m.p.h. When Walt told Tommy that his fast ball wasn't up to par, Tommy wanted to tell him that Randy Jones of the Padres won 22 games with an 80 m.p.h. last fall.

Tommy knew rest wasn't the answer. Rhythm—getting back into the routine of pitching—is what he needed more than anything. He wished for more chances to start, but because of the earlier strike, the additional preseason starts were simply not there.

"You are pitching against the Angels Sunday in Anaheim—Nolan Ryan is starting for them," Walt told Tommy at last.

He was happy and excited about the start. Nolan Ryan, an old friend, was also a pitching nemesis. The press made much of Tommy's "rebuilt" arm and publicized that since Ryan had had surgery over the winter too, it would be a battle between the two "postoperative" arms.

Tommy started the game in a light rain at Anaheim Stadium. Among the thirty thousand fans, nearly fifty friends, neighbors, and people from church came to watch him.

Rain during the baseball season is quite unusual for teams in Southern California. The heavy drizzle made it difficult for both teams and the umpires. When even an exhibition game is started in any kind of rain, it is difficult for an umpire to call a game because of rain. It becomes a matter of judgment as to whether it is raining *more* than it was when the game play began, and no umpire feels he wants to make that kind of decision.

The game was to get under way. The first pitch was the most difficult. It was the one to break the psychological pressure. Everyone was a little tense. The infielders shuffled nervously and slapped their hands to their gloves. Steve Garvey called over encouragement before Tommy started his windup motion. The first inning was a tough one for Tommy. He had a shaky start and was lucky to get out of the inning without a run scoring.

But after that, Tommy settled down. His performance during the next 5 innings was superb. He threw 6 innings of 3-hit, 1-run ball. Alston took Tommy out of the game after the sixth inning for a pinch hitter, but not before Tommy earned the admiration of fans and sportswriters who came to see the comeback of Tommy John.

For his performance that day, Tommy was voted the Lefty Phillips Outstanding Pitcher Award, as the finest effort by a pitcher in the Freeway Series between the Dodgers and the Angels.

Sally was sitting in the stands with her friend, neighbor Bobbi Zink, when the public address announcer told the crowd that Tommy was named the Outstanding Pitcher of the Freeway Series. The two women looked at each other wordlessly. Both hoped now Tommy had really come back. They hugged each other and began to cry, overcome with emotion. They were so thankful.

The 1976 season opened and Tommy was scheduled to pitch in San Francisco. The game was rained out. However, instead of pitching him the next day, manager Alston skipped Tommy in favor of the next pitcher in the rotation. Tommy was upset and frustrated because he was ready and he wanted to pitch.

Back in Los Angeles after the road trip, Tommy was once more scheduled to pitch. Again the rains came to postpone the game. And once more Alston skipped over Tommy.

Tommy finally pitched his first game of the 1976 season in Atlanta after not having pitched in 15 days. He pitched a "respectable" game, as he called it. He went 5 innings and the Dodgers lost 3–1.

Sally listened to the game at home in Yorba Linda with Tami and the German shepherd, Bonnie Blue. Bonnie had proved to be a good investment. Once while Tommy was gone, Sally was awakened by the sound of a screen being removed from a patio window. Immediately Bonnie Blue leaped into action. The dog sprang at the would-be intruder before he could even open the window—which was a blessing for him—since the snarling watchdog could not get at him. Whoever it was was scared away. Sally was frightened, but felt reassured by Bonnie's alertness.

Vin Scully, the Dodger radio and TV announcer, was doing the play-by-play of Tommy's game as Sally listened and Tami, now about seven months old, played with the dog.

"It's not a good night for Tommy John," Vin Scully was saying to listeners. "As you know, he's been giving all he has to a courageous comeback, but you never know. Walt Alston is going to give T. J. just one more chance . . . ."

Sally couldn't believe her ears. The announcer continued. "The Dodgers are going to give Tommy one more time to either prove himself as a starter, or be sent to the bull pen."

Sally sat on the edge of the sofa disbelievingly. There was no mistaking the words. *How unfair!* she thought. *He gave up only 3 runs.* Later, after the team had returned to the hotel and Tommy had called her, she asked him about it.

"Is it true?" she asked Tommy.

"What?"

"That Walt is going to give you just one more chance?"

"W-what?" stammered Tommy. "What are you talking about?"

"I heard on the radio that Walt is going to start you in Houston as your last chance. If you don't prove yourself there, they'll send you to the bull pen!"

There was silence on the other end of the line. Then Tommy answered. "It's the first I heard. If it's true, he hasn't told me. I'll ask him first thing tomorrow. I'm glad you told me! I probably would not have found out until Houston."

"Is it true, Walt?" Tommy asked the next day at the Atlanta Stadium. "I mean the talk of putting me in the bull pen?"

"What? No, of course not," Alston said.

"Well, Sally heard on the radio . . . ."

"Look, we're just adding Rick Rhoden to the lineup. He's ready and we've held him back long enough. You'll start again."

"When?"

"Probably Houston . . ."

"And after Houston?"

"Uh . . . well, let's wait and see," the manager said. "If you get in trouble, well . . . maybe we'll have to use you in the bull pen."

Tommy knew the Dodgers would not use him as a bull pen pitcher. Instead, they'd either release or trade him, if he somehow didn't live up to Alston's expectations.

It didn't matter if Tommy won 20 games after 2 losses. He had to come back after only 1 loss. There'd be just one more chance. He *had* to win to stay as a big league pitcher with the Dodgers.

Tommy called over his friend, catcher Joe Ferguson.

"Joe, ol' buddy. I've got one more chance."

"Yeah, I heard . . ." the catcher replied.

"You've gotta help me, Joe," Tommy said. "In the first game I was doing something wrong . . . bad mechanical habits. I could afford to grope along when I was healthy and troubleshoot those bad habits. But now I've got to straighten them out before Houston."

"Come on," smiled Joe. "Let's get to work."

The two of them began to work out together. Joe helped point out mechanical errors in Tommy's pitching and assess the quality of his different pitches.

"Joe, will you catch for me at Houston?"

"Sure, if it's okay with Walt."

"I'll ask him."

In Houston Alston approved the use of Joe Ferguson as Tommy's catcher. Joe and Tommy decided to "live or die with the fast ball."

There was an unbelievable amount of pressure on Tommy in Houston. As the game got under way, Tommy pitched a hard curve ball for a strike to Wilbur Howard. The second pitch, a slow curve, was a high bouncer over Tommy's head for an infield hit. The second batter, Enos Cabell, hit a ground ball into right field for a base hit.

With runners at first and second, no outs, and Tommy preparing to face the dangerous Cesar Cedeno, Walt Alston called the bull pen to get another pitcher warming up. Tommy then proceeded to get Cedeno to hit a grounder to Bill Russell, the shortstop. The runner on second base sped to third as the shortstop threw to second. The runner on first was forced out but the double play attempt failed as the throw to first was wild. Seeing the wild throw, the runner on third ran for home. Joe Ferguson, the catcher, blocked the plate while waiting for Garvey's throw. The first baseman threw the ball hard to the catcher who caught it and tagged the runner for the second out. Ferguson quickly checked Cabell, now at second, with 2 out.

Houston's clean-up hitter, Bob Watson, was the next batter. Tommy's first three pitches to Watson made the count 3–0. Ferguson called time and hustled out to the mound. "Okay, T.J. Your back is to the wall. Walt's ready to take you out so let's go after Watson with 3 of the best fast balls you have. Let's see what you're made of!"

Expecting ball 4, Watson held his bat as a fast ball whizzed over the plate for a strike.

". . . what I'm made of, huh . . ." Tommy remembered their earlier conversation. He served up two more super fast balls and struck Watson out, swinging. He was out of the inning with no runs scoring. The players congratulated Tommy after the tough inning.

Tommy continued to pitch shut-out ball and left the game in the top of the eighth inning with no runs being scored against him. The score was 0–0. Walt Alston came over to Tommy on the bench and grinned. "It's good to see you've gotten back in the groove, T.J."

Tommy was perplexed and somewhat frustrated that his manager seemed to think his first outing, against Atlanta, was a slump, and that by doing well in his second start he'd "gotten back in the groove." But now, Tommy thought, Walt had resolved that in his mind, he had nothing to prove, and at least for the moment his job was a little more secure.

Tommy returned to Los Angeles with the Dodgers and was scheduled to pitch against Pittsburgh. The Pirates, always noted for their powerhouse hitting, would be a tougher test than Houston.

It was a very emotional time for Tommy, as he walked to the mound that day. It was his home crowd—Dodger fans—that he'd pitch for today. Playing before the home-team crowd excites and motivates a pitcher, and usually draws a better performance than when he's on the road. However, the other side of the coin is not so pleasant. No pitcher enjoys losing face before his home-team fans.

Sally decided not to sit in her regular section for the game. She knew she'd be too emotional—that there would be too much drama to deal with—to sit in the public eye. She decided to sit and watch the game with Bob and Joanie Cohen in their box seats so she could yell, cry, or scream and not be noticed.

The sportswriters, with typewriters ready, were there to see if Tommy was capable to make a comeback. Somehow it seemed ironic to Tommy that he could very easily make a comeback as an outstanding pitcher, but never get a chance to demonstrate his ability. If he did not pitch well this next game, and the next, he'd probably not be used as a starter after that. "His arm never came back," they'd say, even though he had maybe merely had a couple of "off" days.

Tommy went out that day to pitch 7 great innings, working on a shutout. In the top of the eighth inning Tommy allowed back-to-back doubles and the Pirates scored a run.

Walt Alston walked out to the mound, motioning for relief pitcher Mike Marshall to come in and take over. "You've done a fine job, Tommy. I don't want you to overdo it and mess up your arm," he explained.

Proudly, but reluctantly, Tommy walked from the mound toward the Dodger dugout. As one man, the entire forty thousand fans stood to their feet and gave a thunderous standing ovation to Tommy John.

Sally, crying for joy, stood with the crowd and applauded. She had never felt as proud of Tommy as she did right at that moment. And Tommy never felt as good about a pitching performance. He just wished Walt would have let him finish the game. He was all but speechless when the TV reporters later asked him about the crowd's reaction.

"Nobody knows what it's like to hear and experience that standing ovation," he said. "I could *feel* the good wishes of the fans and I knew Sally would be crying. I felt like I could leap over the center field scoreboard!"

Headlines on the sports pages of newspapers the next day read: TOMMY JOHN IS BACK!

He began to gain confidence in his arm and his pitching. He could win or lose on the merits of his pitching ability alone and not some abstract fears about his arm.

Tommy went on to both win and lose ball games that year, ending the season with a 10–10 record. Many times he was taken out of winning games early, affecting the final season results. He had a much better season than the statistics showed.

"The first half of the season was a learning process," he explained to his dad at Christmas. "I had to learn or relearn so many little things about batters, mechanics of pitching, and the like. It was almost like starting over. The last half was spent in regaining my confidence and getting batters out when I had to get them out. The last quarter was a dream. The old confidence was there."

"It's a dream come true, son," his father remarked. "We never dared hope you'd get your arm back—let alone pitch again."

"He was consistent, too," Sally chimed in proudly. "Tommy started in 31 games and pitched 207 innings and earned his top salary increase from the Dodgers. He didn't miss a start."

"And didn't your arm get stronger by the end of the season?" his father asked.

Tommy nodded. "The last quarter of the season I threw the ball as well as I ever have in my life. Of the 6 games I finished this year, 5 of them were from my last 8 starts. I'm really excited about getting started next year. I shut out the Reds 9–0 in Cincinnati in September and that was a big plus for me."

"I'm so proud of Tommy," Sally bubbled. "Not too many people had any confidence in Tommy at all, But he won 10 games that 99.9 percent of the people who knew about it figured he would never win."

People other than Tommy's folks and Sally were likewise impressed with his 1976 comeback performance. He was awarded the Sporting News National League Comeback Player of the Year Award, the Fred Hutchinson Award for Outstanding Character and Courage, and several other awards and certificates of achievement.

There was also an unexpected answer to prayer for Tommy and Sally.

"We prayed for opportunities to share our faith with people we know," Sally reminded Tommy. "God's opened doors like you wouldn't believe. Look at all these letters from people who want to hear your story."

Tommy was asked by civic organizations, Little Leagues, businessmen's luncheons, schools, and churches to come and speak.

Everywhere he went, he told how God gave him the courage and faith to persevere and conquer his handicap. He even spoke for the Braille Institute.

Also at the end of the 1976 season word came that Walt Alston was retiring. It was a sad and emotional event for Dodger fans and the news stunned Los Angeles.

Tommy said, "He'll be missed. He was a major league manager for twenty-three consecutive years. Imagine that! Yes—things will sure be different without Walt. He's really knowledgeable about the game of baseball."

"Who's taking his place?" Sally asked Tommy.

"Tom Lasorda," he answered.

"Is that good?"

"I really think it's a great change. He's on the same wavelength as the players. He'll scream and yell at the umpires and at you. But, above all, he's in your corner giving you a pat on the back.

"In a way, I hate to see Walt leave. I guess that's the conservatism in me. Walt is a true man and a gentleman. He says what he thinks and sometimes we [the players] didn't like it. If he was proved wrong, he would admit it. He was a major league manager for twenty-three years for the top organization in baseball. He was definitely up on the game. He knew exactly what he was doing. Walt is a good friend and will be missed by the Dodgers and by baseball!"

"Will Mr. Lasorda let you pitch?" Sally asked.

Tommy laughed, "We'll see, Sweetheart, we'll see."

12

Superyear

After the dust of the announcement settled, Tom Lasorda called on each Dodger individually. He explained his management ideas and told each man exactly what he and the Dodgers expected of him for the remaining few weeks of the '76 season, and particularly in 1977. Lasorda talked with Tommy and told him to work on getting his arm in shape for the coming season.

"I expect you to pitch every fifth game," Lasorda told him. As if to underscore the point, at Christmas he sent a holiday greeting with the words *I need you* penned with the signature.

Eddie Stanky was the last manager to tell Tommy what was expected of him and then took the time to specifically encourage or help him during the season. Tommy had always appreciated these qualities in Eddie, and that probably is one reason they are such good friends even today. He and Tom Lasorda were off to the same good start, Tommy thought.

The "good start" was short-lived, however. Since Tommy only had a one-year contract with the Dodgers for the 1976 season, it was time for another round of negotiations.

Tommy and Bob collaborated on the meeting with the Dodger management once more. Tommy felt having an attorney handle negotiations was better so that he could concentrate on one thing—baseball. The club relied heavily on statistics to form a basis for their offer. Tommy believed they should also consider potential—especially since his injury had slowed his progress.

"It'll be difficult for us to sell potential," reminded Bob, as he and Tommy prepared for their meeting with Al Campanis. "But if we can convince them, it'll be because Tommy John can prove he can deliver what he says."

The Dodgers were not convinced. They stood firm with their original offer. It was time for spring training to start and still the two sides had not come to terms.

Tommy reported to Vero Beach with the rest of the team with Bob Cohen and Al Campanis still negotiating back and forth on Tommy's contract.

One day Sally overheard a couple of commentators discussing the contract talks.

"I can't believe Tommy John is holding out for a better contract," remarked one, "after all the Dodgers have done for him."

"Yeah," said the other commentator, "they carried him on the pay roster the entire year he was disabled. What more can he expect with a bum arm?"

Until the matter was resolved, Tommy and Sally decided to stay at a nearby Holiday Inn. Tommy felt there was no need to subject Sally to the pressures of contract negotiations and its subsequent fallout among those she considered to be their friends.

About this time Sally learned she was pregnant with their second child. This one bright note happily cancelled out some of the friction caused by Tommy's slow contract discussions.

The press caught wind of some of the contract difficulties and variously portrayed Tommy as the ungrateful villain. Tommy shrugged off the criticism and left the details to Bob Cohen.

There was still no agreement on a contract when the season began. Tommy lost his first game to the Atlanta Braves. It was a sorry disappointment. When he saw Tom Lasorda coming to take him out of the game, he wondered what he'd say.

"Tommy, you're throwing the ball too hard—don't take these things personally," the manager said. He put his arm around Tommy's shoulder and added, "Don't worry about it. Let the Dodgers and your guy work out the contract—you just pitch ball for me, okay? Listen—I want you to know one thing. As long as I'm manager, you're going to pitch every fifth game. You concentrate on that and be ready. Forget what you read in the papers or hear on the street. You're going to pitch for me, T.J., because I want a pennant so bad I can taste it! I want to taste the fruits of victory!"

Tommy's second time out, he pitched to a 5–3 lead before he was relieved in the seventh inning in a game at San Francisco. The next start, at home before Dodger fans, he struck out 8 batters and was relieved by Charlie Hough, who gave Tommy a combined shutout win over Montreal.

His next game, against the New York Mets, was his best effort of the 1977 season to date. He pitched all 9 innings and gave up only 1 run.

Bob Cohen emerged from meetings with Al Campanis with a contract—this time a two-year pact which both sides felt was fair. Once again Tommy and Sally were a part of the Dodger family, and with all the pressures off, Tommy could continue the regular season with excellent performances. The "potential" he had tried to sell now became a game-winning reality.

His rapport with Tom Lasorda grew and the respect each had for the other was evident. In a game at Shea Stadium, behind 2–1, Tommy expected his manager to pull him in a late inning for a pinch hitter.

When Tommy's turn to bat came, he looked over his shoulder to Lasorda to see if the manager had someone to hit for him. But the manager just pointed toward the plate and said, "Go out and get me a hit." Tommy raised his eyebrows. He'd struck out at bat the time before. Now, with two outs and two runners on, even Tommy would have questioned Lasorda's strategy of letting his pitcher bat. However, Tommy responded to the confidence Lasorda had in him. New York pitcher Jerry Koosman delivered the first pitch to Tommy, who lined the ball to right centerfield for a base hit, driving in the tying run. The Dodgers rallied after that to win 7–2. So, instead of a no-decision game, a pinch-hitting situation was turned around because Lasorda showed confidence in Tommy.

Another example of Lasorda's confidence was on display when the Dodgers were playing the Pirates in August. Pittsburgh, perennial contenders, were giving Tommy a rough time when Lasorda walked to the mound. It was the bottom of the ninth with the score 1–1. Two men were on base with 2 outs. Phil Garner came to bat, a dangerous right-handed hitter. Dave Parker, leading hitter of the National League was the next batter.

"I'm going to the bull pen, T.J.," Lasorda said.

"But, Tom, I don't think you should," Tommy answered.

"I want to pitch a right-hander against Garner," Lasorda explained.

Tommy shook his head. "What if he doesn't get Garner? Then who're you going to pitch against Parker?"

"I'll bring in the left-hander," Lasorda answered.

"Shoot—I'd rather pitch against Parker, tired, with the bases loaded and two out, than see my game on the line with a rookie pitching. I believe I can do as well against Parker. He may crush me, but I think I can get him out."

Tom Lasorda pursed his lips and surveyed the situation. He gave Tommy a swat on the seat and said, "That's good enough for me. Go get him—it's your ball game."

Tommy pitched to Garner who hit a ground ball to Bill Russell at shortstop for the third out and kept the Dodgers alive. In the tenth inning the Dodgers went on to score and win the game, 2–1.

Time and time again Lasorda allowed Tommy to stay in and finish a game instead of bringing in a relief pitcher or putting in a pinch hitter. As a result, Tommy's confidence in his own ability grew, and so did the results of his pitching.

Just as Lasorda promised, the manager did not play games with his pitching staff. His promise that Tommy would pitch every fifth game in rotation was kept. Tommy knew exactly where he stood—there were no politics, no seniority, no second-guessing. Lasorda took the pressure off his players and allowed them to tell *him* what the upper level of their achievement could be. As a result, Tommy was off to his best year ever. By the middle of July, his record was 10–4. Following the All-Star break in July, Tommy strung together ten wins to post a 20–7 season.

One game in particular drew national attention. In a much-publicized trade, New York Met pitching great, Tom Seaver, was traded to the Dodgers' archrival, the Cincinnati Reds. Seaver was clearly the favorite in his first game with the Reds. There was unusual pressure on Tommy. Posters all over Cincinnati proclaimed the great Tom Seaver. Sally came along on the road trip. Friends, family, and parents were on hand. Reporters questioned Tommy and if ever he'd cave in, it would be now. However, Tommy John beat Tom Seaver, 3–2, in an amazing performance by the two outstanding pitchers. The year was sailing along smoothly. He was 15–6.

In August, at Dodger Stadium in Los Angeles, Tommy again pitched to the archrival Cincinnati Reds. Rick Ashton, Tommy and Sally's seven-year-old nephew, flew out from Covington, Indiana, to watch his "Uncle Tommy" pitch. The plane got in just in time for them to get to the ball park on time. It was Rick's first game at Dodger Stadium and he was awed and excited.

Young Grant Sullivan, a son of a neighbor of Tommy and Sally, accompanied Rick. At Dodger Stadium, Manager Tom Lasorda welcomed the boys as his own, gave them a tour of his office and the clubhouse. Lasorda introduced the boys to the players and gave them souvenir Dodger batting helmets.

Sally met the wide-eyed youngsters in the family section of the grandstand before the game started. They all sat down to enjoy the game and watch a superb pitching display by Tommy. During the game, Sally—two weeks from her delivery date—got up to go to the rest room. While she was gone, Tommy came to bat. Reds' starting pitcher, Paul Moskau, threw a fast-ball strike which Tommy swung at. As soon as he heard the *crack* of the bat on the ball, Tommy knew it was a well-hit ball right over George Foster's head. It was Tommy's first National League home run and his fifth major league home run. Sally came out of the rest room just in time to hear the cheers.

She looked up at the scoreboard. "Oh, a Dodger home run! Great!" Sally asked a fat man standing next to her, "Who hit it?"

The man blinked and said, "The pitcher—Tommy John!"

Sally screamed and began dancing up and down.

"Hey, lady," the man cautioned, seeing her obvious pregnancy, "calm down!"

"B-but," she stammered, hugging the fan, "that's my husband! I can't *believe* it! I missed his first National League home run!"

Sally hurried back to her seat where friends all kidded her generously. Rick, her young nephew, ran up and hugged her excitedly. "I just saw Uncle Tommy hit a home run!—and against Cincinnati! *Wow* . . . !"

Wow, indeed. Young Rick's excitement could hardly be contained as he watched his Uncle Tommy go on to win the game, a 4–0, 2-hit shutout.

By late August there were two countdowns going. Tommy was going for his first 20-game-win season, and Sally was marking off the days until their second child would be born. It was going to be close as to who would reach their goal first. As it turned out, Sally beat him.

On August 31, her labor contractions began about nine o'clock in the morning. Since the contractions were irregular and not as painful as she recalled them when Tami was born, Sally took her time getting ready. She showered, fixed her hair and nails, then decided to have Tommy drive her to the doctor's office to check and see if she was really in labor stages.

The doctor confirmed her suspicions. "You can go check in at the hospital. It's definitely labor, but you have some time."

Sally asked Tommy to stop at home first to pick up a few things first before leaving for the hospital. Sally then called the ball park while Tommy was getting her things into the car. Red Adams answered the clubhouse phone.

"Red, is it all right if Tommy's late for the game today? He's taking me to the hospital. Today's the big day!"

"Great—let us know as soon as something happens. Are you hoping for a boy this time?" Red asked.

"A boy would be nice," Sally answered. "But if we get another girl like Tami, we'll be happy, too."

"Well, you tell Tommy to take the whole day off. After all he's contributed to the club, he's earned it," declared Red.

On the way to the hospital Sally told Tommy, "You know, we haven't even thought of a girl's name. We had a boy's name picked out from last time, Thomas Edward John III, but what if it's a girl? What will we name her?"

Tommy grinned, "How about some nice biblical name—like Euodias . . . or Syntyche?"

Sally looked at Tommy to see if he was actually serious.

"Okay . . . got any ideas? How about Teresa or Taylor?"

They continued to discuss the possibilities until they got to Saint

Jude's and checked in. That done, they discussed other name ideas until the doctor came by to examine her.

"Your time is getting pretty close," he said. He turned to the nurse, "Take her into the delivery room and prepare her for the epidural."

The nurse wheeled Sally into the delivery room. The obstetrician sat down with Tommy outside the room to finish a Seven-Up before the two of them went in for the delivery.

Suddenly, inside the delivery room they heard a commotion. The physician cocked his head to listen, then stood and hurried inside, calling over his shoulder, "Tommy—you wait here!"

Tommy blinked, aware something seemed wrong.

Inside the delivery room the anesthesiologist was to give an epidural injection to Sally which would merely numb her hips and legs and enable her to watch the birth of her baby, painlessly.

Suddenly, however, she felt an intense flooding seizure in her spine, and quickly shooting up her back to her head—something either freezing cold or scalding hot—she could not tell which. It happened so quickly she tried to gasp—to catch her breath. Her body would not respond. She could sense the life-giving air in front of her face, yet she could not breathe it in!

A nurse called out. There was a clatter of equipment and supplies, as the medics responded to the emergency. Yet, Sally still did not know what was happening. She saw her legs and arms fall off the table and was helpless to stop them. Again she tried to breathe—it was impossible. She couldn't speak or feel or call out to tell anyone she was unable to breathe. She felt dizzy. The room began to darken.

"Get out of the way!" Sally heard her doctor's familiar voice taking charge. She could tell by what he was saying and the choice of language of the anesthesiologist that he was upset at what was happening. "Oxygen! *Now!*" called someone, but his voice getting more distant.

Sally panicked, She had full awareness that she was actually dying on the table before them. Yet, in spite of her fears, she had an inner peace—an assurance that she was going with Jesus to heaven, and knew she would be all right even in death.

Please, God . . . help them save my baby—for Tommy's sake, she prayed. In the microseconds that followed, Sally observed—almost as a spectator—as her life passed before her in some amazing kind of replay. Her childhood, times with her folks, Tommy, and Tami.

With a conscious effort, as she felt her life slipping away, she formed her last thoughts into a peaceful *good-bye* with no regrets.

The room was black now, and voices gone. Her last conscious sight, in the right-hand corner of her field of vision, was that of Jesus: He was depicted exactly as she would expect, in sandals and a white robe. She knew instantly who He was, but didn't know if she was dreaming, or if it was death itself that ushered in this strange new reality.

The obstetrician came out and told Tommy everything was all right. "You can come in now. The baby is about to be born. Sally, however, is unconscious. She'll be okay, but she'll be asleep for a while."

Good-bye, she thought. Then . . . nothingness.

For a moment—or for an eternity—this black void continued. Then Sally was aware of brightness ahead of her. Her journey to heaven was ending. Soon she would be with God and Christ. The brightness was getting more intense. Sally had the sensation of soaring beyond the confines of her body and earth, interrupted by the sensation that she was at once back within her body. The brightness she saw was vivid even through her closed eyes.

With great concentration of will she forced herself to open her eyes. Sally could not tell anything about heaven except that it was bright, too bright for her eyes. Then, as if reading her thoughts, her eyes were shaded from the brightness. She looked into the bearded face of her anesthesiologist.

"It's all right, Sally. You'll be okay," he told her.

I'm not in heaven, she thought. *But what happened?*

"You're on a breathing machine. Don't worry. You'll be all right." The voice anticipated her fears.

As consciousness slowly came to her, Sally tried to remember what happened. She recalled the searing injection and paralysis. Panic once again clouded her thoughts. She was still utterly paralyzed, able only to blink her eyes. She could not breathe or even swallow. Her body was numb and she felt her neck pulled back and positioned for the breathing machine.

Sally was elated to be "back." Her peace at the thought of dying was overshadowed now by her joy at being alive.

She saw a clock which showed the time to be 9:30. Sally remembered it was a little after six when she was taken into the delivery room. *What happened in those three hours? I want to see Tommy . . . Mother . . . What about the baby?* Her thoughts all tumbled out at once. She was frustrated at being unable to speak.

"Your baby is fine," the anesthesiologist smiled, as if knowing her concern. "You had a boy . . . a healthy baby boy."

A baby boy? Sally was torn with racing emotions—happiness and gratefulness that she delivered a son, of course. But she was also frightened—*what happened to me? Why can't I move or talk?* She felt tears well up in her eyes.

Oh, dear God—is it true? Am I permanently paralyzed? Sally's mind was beginning to clear. Her thoughts were racing. Was it because her mind was all she had left? Her body no longer functioned at the command of her brain. She wanted to see Tommy and wished she could call out his name.

Before long another shadow crossed her face. She forced her eyes to open and saw Tommy standing over her. His tall athletic body was bent over with concern and fatigue. His eyes alternated between happy pride and fearful apprehension.

"Y-you're going to be okay, Sweetheart," he assured Sally. "W-when the anesthetic wears off, you'll get your feeling back. I just feel badly because I know how much you wanted to see your baby being born!" he added.

Sally wanted to reach out for Tommy and take him in her arms. She wanted to talk to him, to share her experience with him. But all she could do was manage a quiet moan, a hoarse guttural sound without meaning. Tears overflowed and ran down her cheeks.

"S-shh-h," Tommy whispered. "Just rest." Then he told her proudly, "I saw the baby being born, Sally. It was beautiful. We got our boy—Thomas Edward John III!"

Sally was taken off the oxygen equipment and started to recover her speech. It was slurred at first, and Tommy—who'd been close by all during her ordeal—teased her about it, trying to make her feel better. He knew she must be scared to death.

Sally seemed more comfortable now. Apparently her paralysis was temporary. As least, she prayed that this was the case as she was wheeled into the recovery room.

The seriousness of what had happened had not yet made its impact on Tommy and Sally. They brought the baby for Tommy and Sally to see. The two of them prayerfully savored the quiet intimacy of these first moments with their new son.

The obstetrician came by to check Sally. She had intense headaches. "I'm afraid you'll have to lie perfectly still tonight, flat on your back," the doctor said to her. "It'll be a pretty uncomfortable couple of days."

His words proved to be an understatement. The first night was nearly unbearable for Sally. She tried to take her mind off the painful ordeal by chatting with her roommate, Anna Corby. It was a long, sleepless, and difficult night. They even watched the sun come up.

During the next two days, Sally experienced more pain—an agonizing one which developed in her right arm and shoulder. Nurses applied heat packs to no avail. They tried massaging the painful muscles. Nothing helped. She could not lift her right arm. The doctor could only prescribe stronger pain medication. Sally knew the pains of childbirth contractions were mild by comparison. She couldn't comfortably nurse her baby or hold him properly. She worried about what effect the medication might have on her milk supply.

By Friday, Sally thought it might help her spirits to see visitors and they came in what the nurses felt were endless streams. Because of the many visitors, they gave Sally her own room. Plants and flowers filled the room. Their close friends Tom and Vickie Trenkmann, Sharon Hough, Nancy Hefley, Ginger and Burt Hooton (Burt was Tommy's road-trip roommate), Jo and Laura Lasorda, Mike and Robin Sweet, Sue Mock and Diane and Bob Stow, Patty Carlson, and neighbor Ed Varvello came by with congratulations, as did dozens of other friends and the pastor from the church as well as friends from the neighborhood. Phone calls never seemed to stop.

Her spirits were revived to see the concern and interest of so many.

Sally, with pain still in her arm, was anxious to go home on Saturday, but the doctor said she couldn't leave the hospital until Sunday evening. Tommy pitched that day and won his seventeenth game of the season. Sally listened to the game and Tommy's postgame interview to hear her husband dedicate the win to their new son, Tommy John III.

Tommy began to relax when he saw Sally at home with their new baby. Now he could concentrate on his goal of 20 wins, something every pitcher dreams of. His 19th win was an important victory. He pitched in San Francisco to beat the Giants, 3–1 on September 19, and clinched the National League Western Division title for the Dodgers. The TV cameras and lights pushed into the clubhouse after the game to watch Tommy's teammates douse him in the traditional champagne ritual.

In Houston, on September 25—exactly three years to the day of his arm surgery—Tommy pitched and won his 20th game. It was a proud and exciting event. Following the game, Tommy called Sally.

"Tami and I watched you on TV," she yelled across the miles. "You were terrific! We're very proud of you! Your son even watched you!"

Reporters called for interviews after that, and even the national media picked up on "Tommy John—the Dodger with the bionic arm." It was indeed a miraculous comeback. Tommy and Sally always paused during those hectic days to thank God for His goodness. Occasionally Tommy was even given the opportunity to praise the Lord before millions of TV viewers or newspaper readers.

"You've been pitching in the majors fourteen years, when most pitchers are ready to quit. Yet you seem to be getting stronger and better," a reporter asked him one day.

"Well," Tommy replied with a grin, "I figure I've got a good seven or eight years to go—as long as I keep my legs in shape. You see, most guys have arm trouble after pitching that many years, but I have a new ligament that has only been used in baseball for two years. God has given me a brand-new arm and it's stronger than ever!"

The newspapers picked up on this comment and got good mileage out of the "bionic arm" slant and Tommy's faith in God.

Pete Rose, ace hitter for the Reds, wisecracked, "It was all right for the doctors to transplant a new arm on Tommy—but did they have to use the arm of Sandy Koufax?"

Tommy, after achieving his 20-win season, however, did not relax. From the time he left Houston, his mind was on the play-off games with the National League Eastern Division winner, Philadelphia.

Tom Lasorda announced that Tommy would get the honor of pitching the first game of the play-offs in Los Angeles. The play-off games consisted of the best of five in a series that would decide the pennant for the National League.

Sally, her parents, and Tommy's folks sat in the stands that day, recalling their terrible memories of the day in 1974 when Tommy threw out the first pitch of the play-offs, right-handed, with his pitching arm in a cast, thinking that Tommy might never play major league baseball again. But God had overruled. It was a rare, dramatic, and emotional moment. Sally was shaking so much that she could hardly hold her movie camera steady, and she wanted so much to capture this important moment.

"Here, Sally," said Gloria Yeager softly. She noticed Sally's moist eyes and shaking hands and offered her assistance. "Let me film this for you," Gloria smiled. The Dodgers lost the first game on fielding mistakes but won the second on excellent playing by the infielders and pitching by Don Sutton.

The play-offs swung to Philadelphia. Sally's parents were in from Indiana to baby-sit so she could accompany Tommy to Philadelphia.

In the third game of the series, the Dodgers won an exciting contest. They were down to 2 outs in the ninth inning and bounced back to win. It was now Dodgers 2, Phillies 1 in the best 3 out of 5 series.

Lasorda announced that Tommy John would pitch the fourth game of the play-offs. It was a nationally televised NBC game, as were the others, except that this event was played in a drizzling rain, unusual for baseball. However, Tommy was not intimidated by the weather, nor the powerful Phillies hitters, nor their ace pitcher, Steve Carlton. Al Campanis watched with a glowing sense of satisfaction that his decision to carry Tommy was the right one as his pitching protégé struck out Bake McBride, the last Philly batter.

He won the game 4 to 1—and the pennant—for the Dodgers, even getting a base hit in the process. That night Tommy and Sally received congratulations in a phone call from singer Frank Sinatra and Don Rickles as the team was celebrating at Tom Lasorda's and his brother's restaurant in Exton, Pennsylvania.

Playing in the World Series with the American League Champion New York Yankees after that was, to use Sally's expression, "frosting on the cake." The games were televised, this time by ABC. Several days before the series, ABC sent a TV crew to Tommy's home in Yorba Linda and videotaped an interview to be used as an insert on the day he was to pitch. It was a chat with Tommy, Sally, and Tami seen by tens of millions of people in America. They watched with interest as Tommy told Howard Cosell and millions of viewers the story of his injury and subsequent comeback, giving the credit for his remarkable achievements to God.

Viewers across the United States could see in his face and by Sally's expression, that his words were not mere patter or false humility. His sincerity and faith registered as genuine, and his experience an inspiration to literally thousands.

The Yankees won the '77 series. Here's a brief summary of the games:

1st game   Don Sutton opened for Dodgers and the Yankees countered with Don Gullett. Both pitched very well and the Yankees won in extra innings, 4–3.

2nd game   Burt Hooton, Tommy's roommate, pitched against Catfish Hunter and the Dodger hitters bombed Hunter with home runs and "Hoot" pitched a great game.

3rd game   Tommy pitched against Mike Torrez. The Yankees scored 3 runs in the first inning and the Dodgers came back to tie the game. Yankees won the game on some bouncing infield hits.

4th game   Doug Rau pitched against Ron Guidry. The Yankees outplayed the Dodgers and won 3–2.

5th game   A match-up of the 1st game with Sutton and Gullett. Sutton pitched a complete game victory 10–4.

6th game   Pitted Burt Hooton against Mike Torrez and it was to be Reggie Jackson's game. Jackson hit the ball the way Tommy remembered him in the American League in the latter 60s. The Yankees outplayed the Dodgers for the world championship, but Tommy would not trade the Dodgers for the Yankee team. The Dodgers just happened to play poorly at the wrong time. People tend to forget that they beat some great clubs to get to the World Series. It was an honor just to be there, Tommy felt.

Soon after the Series, the results of the Cy Young Award balloting were announced. Tommy and Sally were at the hospital visiting Sally's father, who was recovering from a heart attack. They were all elated to learn Tommy had finished second in the voting, just behind Steve Carlton of Philadelphia. It was another honor for which Tommy was more grateful than proud.

There were, of course, a lot of accounts in the media about this newest recognition which had come to Tommy. Ross Newham of the *Los Angeles Times* was to say this about him:

> As a member of the media I am supposed to be dispassionate, unemotional, objective. I am thought of as a cynic, a skeptic, a disbeliever. And I suppose I'm a little of all those things except in the case of Tommy John, whose remarkable comeback destroyed all the facades.
>
> I think, in fact, I can speak for the media as a whole when I say that it is impossible to be dispassionate or unemotional when reflecting on Tommy's comeback. His was a textbook lesson in courage, conviction, belief and determination. The comeback for all seasons. The quintessential example for those victims of a temporary setback or handicap.
>
> In addition, Tommy's comeback is more than the story of a unique operation, more than the chronicle of an athlete's

spirited bid to resume his career. It is the story of how this man refused to permit adversity from changing what he was, what he had always been, as a person. Accessible. Engaging. Courteous. Willing to discuss any subject at any time. A media favorite prior to the injury, he remains just that.

No—dispassion, unemotion, cynicism, skepticism are for other events, other people, other places. They are not for someone who saw Tommy walk off the mound at Dodger Stadium on July 17, 1974, who saw his left arm in bandages during that long winter, who saw his left hand atrophied into the shape of a claw during the longer summer of '75, who saw him pitch again for the first time in an Arizona Instructional League game in the spring of '76. They are not for someone who has known Tommy John, the athlete, the person.

Jack Kinder, a Dallas businessman and friend of Tommy, saw what the arm injury did for Tommy and Sally. "Many times the worst things that happen can turn out to be the best thing for you," he told Tommy one day.

"I've seen how you have grown spiritually after that injury brought you up short. It just goes to show that when things go badly, you can cave in with them, or overcome them. You found the seed of opportunity in what was hopeless adversity. Not everyone can do that. But you, Tommy, sure have given a lot more people hope and courage because *you've* done it!"

"Looking back," Tommy tells audiences, "my experience has been worth every hard moment that was spent. God has used my injury to teach me so much about faith, love, and His power. But we've also had the privilege of watching Him use my experience to help others. He gives us opportunities to share our faith and Christian testimony in ways we never dreamed possible. We're really grateful and praise Him for His goodness."

Press Conference

(EDITOR'S NOTE *The following are questions that are often asked of Tommy John.*)

QUESTION   *What is your routine on the days you pitch?*

TOMMY   Well, on the road I generally sleep late. I try to keep my "biological clock" on Los Angeles time. When I'm pitching, I'll get up about eleven, have a big breakfast, and walk around the hotel, maybe window shopping downtown at the stores.

A couple of hours before the game, I go back to the hotel to rest and think about my game plan. I know a lot of guys are using hypnosis, TM, and other fad ideas, but I prefer to read the Bible and think about what Scripture says. Then I sort of rehearse in my mind how I'm going to pitch to each batter. I visualize Pete Rose or Joe Morgan at the plate, and I try to think of times in the past when I've pitched to them *successfully*. I file that away until the game. I have an idea of what pitches I want to use on each batter—the perfect pitch for every hitter. I also pray for wisdom and guidance to enable me to be a Christian witness in the game—to be a Christian on the field and off— praying for strength much like Jesus prayed in Gethsemane.

About four or five o'clock, I have something to eat that's high in carbohydrates and leave for the ball park.

At home, the routine is pretty much the same. The night before I have steak or a high protein dinner. I work in the yard instead of walking. I mow the lawn and swim about ten minutes on the days I pitch, to work off nervous energy. Then I shower and have lunch—usually spaghetti, a green salad, cake, ice

169

cream, or a milk shake—carbohydrates for quick energy during the game.

On the way to Dodger Stadium, on the days I pitch, I usually ride with Burt Hooton (my roommate on the road). The hour or so it takes to ride is generally the time for me to take a nap. During my quiet time at the ball park, I think about my pitching and spend time in prayer before going out.

QUESTION   *You mention prayer as a part of your routine. Do you think prayer really works?*

TOMMY   I *know* it does. The very fact that I can even move my hand and fingers today is testimony to the power of prayer. Forget about my being able to pitch—just moving my hand is an answer to the prayers of many people: Sally, my folks, her folks, our church. Some people were astonished that God would answer a prayer like this, but I'm not. I think He grants any legitimate request. At least that's what it says in the Bible (John 14:13, 14).

QUESTION   *What do you feel is your responsibility to fans or the public?*

TOMMY   I feel responsible to give the fans and baseball something, and not just take the good things baseball provides for me. That's why I feel compelled to turn in the very best performance I'm capable of.

I also feel ballplayers should set a positive example for youngsters. Children want someone to look up to. If they are looking at a ballplayer as an idol, I think that a ballplayer should live a life-style he'd want his children, or any children, to follow. I guess that's why I'm always willing to sign autographs, or talk to youngsters and let them know about my being a Christian ballplayer. Christianity has values and ideals that are very compatible with sports. Both demand that we do our very best. There's a fine line between success and failure and I believe strongly that my Christianity makes the difference in my life. And because of my relationship to Christ, I feel I have a responsibility to live a Christian life-style that is pleasing to Him.

QUESTION   *Regarding success—do you pray for success?*

TOMMY   A lot of people get confused about this. They hear me talk about prayer and right away they think I pray to win every time I get on the mound. It's not so.

I believe a team will win about a third of their games no matter what, and—by the same token, they'll *lose* a third of them.

It's what a team does with that other third that makes the difference. I pray that God will *help me do my best* with the talent He gave me—that's all. *I* have to put the effort into making that other one-third successful.

QUESTION   *Do you feel any pressures keeping up with social or celebrity life-style demands?*

TOMMY   Sally says living in Los Angeles has really been a thrill for her because she's such a Hollywood fan. She and I have been on TV shows like "Gambit," "Tattletales," and "Hollywood Squares." We have many friends in the entertainment industry, including Bill Anderson, Bob Newhart, Lee Majors, Don Rickles, Glen Campbell, and Ron Masac.

But we don't have many parties, and when we do, we usually have two or three couples over for dinner. Our idea of fun is having some couples over for hot chocolate and doughnuts, or popcorn and cider, sitting around the fireplace talking. We also like to go out and play miniature golf, or go to a good play. We spend a lot of time on the golf course, because I play in a lot of tournaments during the off-season.

We follow our own life-style and don't feel pressures of keeping up with anyone else.

QUESTION   *Does Sally ever wish you were in some other line of work?*

TOMMY   Baseball is a hard life for the wife of a ballplayer. But Sally feels it has rewards that make it worthwhile. She's heard people say, "I'd never want my daughter to marry a baseball player."

But she says, "Where else could a wife go and be with her husband? You meet fantastic people everywhere you go, through baseball. It's a very exciting life and the good far outweighs any bad points. I love meeting wives of players on other clubs. Carolyn Rose was so nice, as was Nancy Seaver. I love it and I'll be behind Tommy to help him continue as long as he can.

"The Dodgers emphasize the family. They are so nice to us (the children and me). Al Campanis even gave the wives beautiful World Series charms in 14k gold. They have Easter egg hunts and Christimas parties for our children. It is very lonely when our guys are on the road, but it makes coming home so much nicer. The money is great, too. Baseball has given us a lot, and especially satisfaction of the "challenge" to my husband.

"The traveling is fantastic. Before the children arrived, I made almost every road trip. The Dodgers have their own plane and allow the wives along if there are extra seats. They are just a first-class organization. The season is long, but we have October through February to ourselves. We love it."

QUESTION   *Did you ask the Dodgers to tear up your contract and negotiate a new one after your great 1977 season record?*

TOMMY   No. I believe a contract should be honored. If it was fair before, then it should be fair now. I think a man should honor his word. I'd never go back on my word and ask the Dodgers to renegotiate a new contract. Some players do, but I disagree. Once I sign a contract, I will honor it.

QUESTION   *Do you feel being a Christian limits you in what you'd like to do?*

TOMMY   I have as much fun being a Christian as someone who doesn't believe as I do. I enjoy material things—a fine home, great family, nice clothes—but I know they are gifts from God. So I try not to take them for granted.

I don't feel the need to dull my senses with drugs or getting drunk, because life is so exciting and stimulating in itself.

I enjoy sex, too, but within my marriage commitment to Sally.

Sure the Bible sets limits and establishes boundaries, but I feel that's a good thing. I'm perfectly happy within these boundaries. The guidelines which Jesus Christ lays out in the Bible are not a set of sour commandments, but standards for a happy, contented life. Just as baseball is easier when you know the rules and play by them, so is the Christian life when you live by the Bible and God's code.

QUESTION   *What role does ego play in a ballplayer's life?*

TOMMY   Ego is a very human trait. And it's a quality that keeps a ballplayer going. In a sense, we're all entertainers out there, performing for the crowds. The fans "hype" your ego. It's very rewarding to sense the adulation of the crowd, the roaring applause. L.A. fans are the best in the country. They are always behind you.

QUESTION   *Do you think Little League is good for youngsters?*

TOMMY   My argument with youngsters playing in various leagues is with the parents and coaches. They are giving the youngsters so much pressure that they aren't having any fun. They are afraid of losing.

Playing baseball as a youngster should be fun. Instead of naming the best athletes as pitcher, catcher, and first baseman, they should rotate the positions. Little Leaguers should play all the positions and not be forced so much by adults. I've seen some youngsters who'll never make it to the major leagues becaue they're all burned out by high school. And that's what upsets me. My dad taught me these concepts when he coached Little League and Babe Ruth League baseball, and I believe it's a great philosophy—and probably one of the reasons I made it to the big leagues. But my father's sacrificial attitude in working with me is the one big factor that got me where I am. I owe a great deal to my dad. I hope I can be half the father to my children that my dad was to me.

QUESTION   *Do you chart your pitches as some others do?*

TOMMY   I don't, but Sally has kept score for every game I've pitched for the Dodgers. She knows whether I pitched a ground-ball out, a strikeout. She's recorded every pitch to every batter. I look at these records and check for things to help my pitching.

QUESTION   *Is it true that you enjoy golf?*

TOMMY   That's a favorite subject, for sure! I love it. I play as
often as I can, especially during the off-season. I try to play in
the Bing Crosby Pebble Beach Tournament as well as several
other Pro-Am events.

In 1977 I started my own charity tournament, the Tommy
John Celebrity Tournament to raise money for the Cystic Fibrosis Foundation. We arranged for entertainers and sports celebrities to team up with golfers and had a great time, raising
money for a great cause. We raised over twenty-six thousand
dollars in the first tournament. I'm presently chairman of the
Southern California Chapter of Cystic Fibrosis and devote time
to helping them raise money.

QUESTION   *What do you plan to do when you retire from
baseball?*

TOMMY   Well, first I hope to complete twenty years in the major
leagues before I step down. After that, we'll just have to see. I
believe God has something in mind for me that will be just as
great as baseball is right now. I have many interests. I love
baseball. Maybe a coaching assignment. But I also enjoy the
communications field and would consider some kind of televi-
sion or film assignment. Sally worked in TV and radio before we
were married, and I know she'd love to get back into the field,
when our youngsters are in school. I enjoy working with people.
I'm sure a lot of things fall into that category. We'll just have to
wait and see what comes our way.

Biography

THOMAS EDWARD JOHN, JR., born May 22, 1943, in Terre Haute, Indiana.

Married Sally Simmons, July 13, 1970.

Two children, Tamara (Tami) Marie, born September 27, 1974, and Thomas (Tommy) Edward III, born August 31, 1977.

Graduated Gerstmeyer High School, Terre Haute, Indiana.

Attended Indiana State University.

Military Service: Indiana Air National Guard.

Baseball Statistics

Year	Club	G	GS	CG	IP	H	BB	SO	W	L	ERA
1961	Dubuque	14	13	4	88	74	59	99	10	4	3.17
1962	Charleston	21	20	7	128	129	71	114	6	8	3.87
1962	Jacksonville	8	7	1	34	29	16	27	2	2	4.76
1963	Charleston	12	12	8	95	85	12	45	9	2	1.61
1963	Jacksonville	18	14	4	102	115	39	63	6	8	3.53
1963	Cleveland	6	3	0	20	23	6	9	0	2	2.25
1964	Cleveland	25	14	2	94	97	35	65	2	9	3.91
1964	Portland	13	11	5	74	75	24	72	6	6	4.26
1965	Chicago	39	27	6	184	162	58	126	14	7	3.09
1966	Chicago	34	33	10	223	195	57	138	14	11	2.62
1967	Chicago	31	29	9	178	143	47	110	10	13	2.47
1968	Chicago	25	25	5	177	135	49	117	10	5	1.98
1969	Chicago	33	33	6	232	230	90	128	9	11	3.25
1970	Chicago	37	37	10	269	253	101	138	12	17	3.28
1971	Chicago	38	35	10	229	244	58	131	13	16	3.62
1972	Los Angeles	29	29	4	187	172	40	117	11	5	2.89
1973	Los Angeles	36	31	4	218	202	50	116	16	7	3.10
1974	Los Angeles	22	22	5	153	133	42	78	13	3	2.59
1975	Los Angeles				(On disabled list)						
1976	Los Angeles	31	31	6	207	207	61	91	10	10	3.09
1977	Los Angeles	31	31	11	221	225	50	123	20	7	2.78

Lifetime won–lost record: American League, 84–91; National League 70–32.

175